UNDERSTANDING GOD'S PROGRAM FOR THE AGES

UNDERSTANDING GOD'S PROGRAM FOR THE AGES

A Study of Dispensations and Covenants

By

Kenneth G. Symes

ARPress
ILLUMINATING IDEAS
EMPOWERING VOICES

ARPress
45 Dan Road Suite 36
Canton MA 02021

Hotline: 1(888) 821-0229
Fax: 1(508) 545-7580

Ordering Information:
Quantity Sales. Special discounts are available on quantity purchases by corporations, associations, and others. For details, contact the publisher at the address above.

Printed in the United States of America.

ISBN-13   Paperback   979-8-89330-657-6
            eBook   979-8-89330-656-9
            Hardback   979-8-89356-198-2

Library of Congress Control Number: 2024902933

"All Bible quotations are taken from The King James Version"

Contents

ACKNOWLEDGEMENTS

A man is truly blessed when he has three things: a relationship with his Creator; a wife who loves and understands him; and friends who are saturated in the word who care enough about you to share their honest and positive criticism with you. I am such a blest man! My wife has been greatly supportive as I have worked through the writing of this book. I have much appreciated my pastor, Dr. John Williamson, who has taken the time to read my manuscript keeping me straight, and helping me to write with clarity. I know of no other layman who is more versed in God's word with understanding of its truth than is Terry Moffitt who has been a faithful critic. I am also grateful to pastor N. A. Thompson III and his dear wife for the assistance they gave in making this effort the best that we can offer. Thanks to Robert DeRespino for his assistance in the formation of the charts found in this book.

This book is the result of a team effort. I am grateful for their help, counsel and encouragement through the process of writing it. May our Lord be glorified in this presentation of His truth with lives changed because of it.

FORWARD

No doubt you have heard the statement, "But that's your interpretation." It is often said when dealing with the scriptures. The Bible nowhere gives us the right or privilege to determine its interpretation by our own prejudices or reasonings. The word of God is its own best interpreter. It is becoming clearer in Christendom that more and more preachers and teachers are failing to abide by one basic rule in their interpretation of the Bible. That rule is: *The Golden rule of interpretation* by Dr. David L. Cooper, the late founder of the Biblical Research. Thoughtful and biblical presentation of that rule has solidified my understanding of the word of God and I am eternally grateful. The rule is this: *"When the plain sense of Scripture makes common sense, seek no other sense; therefore, take every word at its primary, ordinary, usual, literal meaning, unless the facts of the immediate context, studied in the light of related passages and axiomatic (self-evident) and fundamental truths, indicate clearly otherwise."* This is the literal interpretation of scripture. That includes the normal uses of the figures of speech in any language.

We are seeing a prevailing number of Christian leaders who ignore or reject the dispensational view of the Bible. The result has been a mixture of confusing and contradicting ideas being promoted. The main consequence has been the idea that God is finished with Israel, leading to the disturbing anti-Israel attitude prevalent today. Thus, all the promises predicted of Israel's future are now supposedly being fulfilled in the church. The literal interpretation of scripture confirms the fact that God has not abandoned His chosen people. It leads to the view that is presented in this book, that the Bible's revelation is progressive. When one sees God's word through the understanding of the dispensations and covenants, it leads to that compelling understanding the Lord intends. Though there are distinctive aspects in the flow of biblical history, we must understand that God has never saved anyone except by grace through faith. An accurate dispensational view does not promote different ways of salvation. He gives it, we receive it. The dispensational view affirms to us that god's plan for the ages leads to a proper conclusion of human history, not just the redemption of man, but by bringing glory to God. It further settles forever the enmity of God's greatest antagonist, Satan, and his control over God's marvelous creation. Dispensationalists understand clearly that in the end, God wins, Satan loses.

Ken Symes has simplified this view of the scriptures in this book and makes it understandable to laymen in the pew. That is a great service and I am so grateful to the Lord for leading him to write this book. It is not exhaustive, but easily read, and makes the span of biblical history clear and definitive. Having known Ken for more than thirty years, I am grateful to the Lord for his ministry of reaching God's chosen people.

N. A. Thompson III

INTRODUCTION

There are some things that are absolutely necessary for us to understand when we come to the study of God's Word, the Bible. Most people think they just need to pick it up, read it, and they will understand it. After all, the Holy Spirit is our teacher. Others say that we just need to take it literally. To this I fully agree. However, for us to read it and take it literally there are still some matters that the reader needs to understand if he Is to fully receive its wonderful message and instructions for life.

First the reader of the Bible must understand that God's revelation is progressive. In other words, God did not give all of His revelation to Adam and Eve. Some would say that this gave the serpent the opportunity to suggest to Eve that God was holding out. When Eve told him that God had instructed them not to eat of the forbidden fruit he responded: "Ye shall not surely die: *for God doth know that in the day ye eat thereof, then your eyes shall be opened, and ye shall be as gods, knowing good and evil.*" (Genesis 3:4-5). The serpent stated that God was holding out on them, that there was more to know. And if they would just eat the fruit they would become as gods, implying that they would know all truth. He said that they would become as gods but they did not. That was the serpent's second lie. His first lie was when he said they would not die. They did die, first spiritually (Genesis 3:8-10) and then physically.

Was this not the truth of which Isaiah spoke when he said: *"Whom shall he teach knowledge? and whom shall he make to understand doctrine* (truth)? *them that are weaned from the milk, and drawn from the breasts. For precept must be upon precept; line upon line, line upon line; here a little, and there a little."* (Isa. 28:9-10) (cf. Chart #2). Clearly he shows that teaching (revelation) is progressive, related to how much the recipient is able to receive at any given time. Isaiah also shows us that truth is built on truth, precept upon precept. So there are basic truths upon which other truths are built. Thus, before one can move forward in his understanding of biblical truth he must first grasp an understanding of the foundational truths (Hebrews 5:12-6:1; II Peter 3:18).

This book is written to help the reader grasp the foundational truths of God's Word so that he may move forward to understand the broader truths of His Word. It is our goal to establish for you the umbilical cord of God's progressive revelation from which all other truths develop. Having this foundation the Bible will come alive to become the guide and strength God forever intended it to be for His children.

This study is intended to accomplish one other matter. Everyone, whether they think of it in these terms or not, has a world view. This is the basis upon which we understand the world and its history. Upon completing this study the reader will know that God is in control of His creation which includes this world. Developing a solid biblical world view will enable the reader to discern the lies regarding any other world view that is being proposed. Remember, Satan and his ambassadors are, even today, proposing a diametrically opposed world view. Through this study you will understand that history only makes sense in the light of God and His clearly laid out plan for the ages. This will help you develop a positive view of the future, enabling you to make right decisions according to God's eternal plan. In other words, the reader will develop a true biblical world view as well as the foundation necessary to fully understand and appreciate the Bible, God's love letter to mankind.

This book is about the flow of God's progressive revelation and of history. Since the 1600's there has developed what has become two very distinct approaches to developing a biblical philosophy of history. The one is Covenant Theology and the other is Dispensationalism. Most, in either theological camp, see their view as exclusive of the other. Those who embrace Covenant theology focus on two covenants, a covenant of works and a covenant of Grace. They do not follow the rule of verbal inspiration which necessitates taking Scripture as verbally inerrant. Dispensationalists, on the other hand, hold to the doctrine of verbal inerrancy and thus are driven by the necessity to take Scripture literally. Dispensationalists accept that there are eight biblical Covenants that establish God's plan for the ages as well as seven dispensations. In this study we shall see that the Bible teaches that God's plan for the ages uses both covenants and dispensations. Thus, if we are to be biblical in our theological framework, we must accept that the Bible teaches both covenants and dispensations and recognize that, as they are not in conflict with one another, they actually complement one another. One purpose of this study is to help the reader understand both biblical covenants and dispensations and how they fit together in one grand plan.

Our intention in this book is to help the reader understand what the Bible clearly teaches regarding covenants and dispensations. As the Bible is the source of all truth, should not whatever system of theology we develop be based upon God's Word in such a manner as to not create any contradictions of those truths? It is our purpose to simply show what the Bible clearly teaches.

Finally, this study will strengthen the reader's understanding that the Bible, including both Old and New Testaments, is one book, complete and without error or contradiction. We will show that dispensations and covenants are biblically compatible destroying what has become in our time, a theological straw man; showing that God has always had just one plan for the ages which He is presently working out toward its ultimate completion in history, a plan that includes both covenants and dispensations.

CHAPTER 1

FOUNDATIONS I

God's revelation to mankind was delivered progressively, that is, in steps or increments. His revelation of truth is as a river that starts with a spring and develops into a large flowing river. The spring from which all truth flows is found in Genesis chapters 1-3. Here we note that God started with some very basic truths which were shared with Adam in the garden. There are three fundamental truths that constitute the spring from which all biblical truth is developed.

The first foundational truth is that the eternal God is the source of all creation and life (Gen. 1:1). This truth is then detailed in Genesis 1:2 to 2:3 where we are instructed on the process of creation. In Genesis 2:4-15, 18-25 we are given a more detailed account of the activities of the sixth day relating to the creation of man. This is the foundation of every other truth found in the Bible.

The second foundational truth is that God established a relationship between man and Himself. God created man in His own image giving to man a free will (Genesis 2:16-17). This was essential because God wanted a relationship with man that was based upon the free choice of both parties. This relationship was to embody the free flow of love from God to man and from man to God. The only meaningful relationship we as humans can have is when a relationship is based upon two people choosing freely and unconditionally to love one another. God could have created man to simply be a puppet. But that would not have given any real satisfaction to either God or the man He was going to create. It would be like a human having a doll or teddy bear. There is a time when a child will love the doll or teddy bear. But as time goes on, this becomes an unsatisfactory relationship because the doll or teddy bear cannot love the child in return. Satisfaction in a relationship comes from love flowing in both directions between two people. It was God's intent that man have a meaningful relationship with Him. That could only be possible if man was free to choose to have and maintain a caring relationship with God. This is a fundamental truth that determines how God would deal with man for all eternity.

The third foundational truth is the principle of redemption established by God because of man's fall (Gen. 3:15). This principle established the promise of a redeemer who would free us from the just penalty of our sins. He would be the perfect God-man who would ultimately exchange His perfect life as a sacrifice for our sins. The establishment of this "exchange of life" principle is made clear when God exchanged the coverings of leaves Adam and Eve made for themselves to hide their nakedness (the work of their own hands) with coats of skins which necessitated the killing of innocent animals (Genesis 3:21). This understanding is further underlined in Genesis chapter four as it becomes clear that Adam and Eve taught their sons that they were to approach God only through a blood sacrifice (the "exchange of life" principle). Abel offered an acceptable sacrifice. Cain offered fruit from his fields which were unacceptable because they represented self effort. When God spoke to Cain about his unacceptable sacrifice He said: *"If thou doest well, shalt thou not be accepted?"* (Genesis 4:7). This clearly indicated that Cain knew what was required of him. Upon these three truths flows all biblical truth.

As biblical truth is progressive, how then are we to understand God's Word? A stream or river flows between two banks. From this major flow there are other streams and tributaries. The only difference is that in the practical world the streams and tributaries feed the river. Whereas, in understanding God's revelation we must understand that it is the river which feeds the streams and tributaries.

THE RIVER BANKS

There is an interesting fact that few have recognized that shows there is a significant relationship between biblical covenants and dispensations. A serious study of the Bible will show that the first four covenants parallel the first four dispensations. The Edenic Covenant parallels the Dispensation of Innocence. The Adamic Covenant parallels the Dispensation of Conscience. The Noahic Covenant parallels the Dispensation of Government, while the Abrahamic Covenant parallels the Dispensation of Promise (cf. chart #1). The Mosaic, Palestinian and Davidic Covenants fall within the Dispensation of the Law in time only, not in quality or duration. The New Covenant parallels the Dispensation of Grace, while both conclude with the Dispensation of the Millennium. In this study we will explain all of the biblical covenants and dispensations and demonstrate their relationship to each other. However, at this point we are simply seeking to establish the basic relationship between them. As we continue further into this study, we will begin to recognize that God's progressive revelation flows between the biblical covenants as one bank of the river and biblical dispensations as the other bank (cf. Chart # 2).

DISPENSATIONAL DEFINITIONS

It is important to understand that God's purpose for covenants and dispensations are different. In developing our understanding of biblical dispensations, there are three biblical terms that we need to define and understand. The first is "dispensation". In the Bible the word that is translated "dispensation" four times is *oikonomia*. In its sixteen other appearances it is translated "steward" or "stewardship". A dispensation is characterized by two parties: the one who delegates the duties and the one responsible for carrying out those duties. In this arrangement, in which God is the one delegating the duties with man as the one responsible for carrying out the duties, there is always a specific test that establishes accountability. The test changes from time to time and is related to God's developing or progressive revelation of truth. But the tests are never contradictory.

A dispensation involves a specific time frame determined by God. The ending of one dispensation and the beginning of another often involves the annulment of certain duties and the establishment of new ones. But God's plan for the redemption of man never changes. There is now, and always has been, only one way to be saved which was established by God immediately after Adam and Eve rebelled against God's authority. Charles Ryrie correctly states: "What marks off the various economies in the outworking of God's purpose and distinguishes each from the other is twofold: (1) the different governing relationship with the world into which God enters in each economy; and (2) the resulting responsibility on mankind in each of these different relationships. Thus a dispensation is an act of administration or the management of an estate."i The estate, in biblical terms, is the world. The administrator is God. The responsibilities are delegated to man. As we shall see through this study, God administers His estate in a very clear and definitive way.

The second word of importance to this study is "ages". There are two words used in the Bible that are translated "ages" in our English Bible. The first is aion translated "ages" in Ephesians 2:7 and Colossians 1:26. This word literally means: relative time duration, limited or unlimited. If this relates to a dispensation it is clear by the context, for example see Colossians 1:26. The second word is *genea* (Ephesians 3:5, 21) which means a generation or a specific time period. An "age" is here defined as a specific period of time that has significant character (an era). *Oikonomia* (dispensation) emphasizes stewardship whereas *aion* and *genea* refer to the period of time.

The words "dispensation" and "ages" (*genea*) are interchangeable in the biblical record (cf. Ephesians 3:1-5. 21). Both words, as they relate to one another, may be defined as: A period of human history wherein man is given specific stewardship responsibilities, expressed in terms of Divine revelation, which is divine categories of human history, or the Divine viewpoint of human history. So the emphasis of dispensations is on the time period. Each dispensation, as we shall learn through this study, may be regarded as a test of the natural man with each test ending in judgment marking man's utter failure.

WHY STUDY DISPENSATIONS?

There are at least four reasons why the student of the Bible should study dispensations. First, we need to study dispensations because the Bible was given in increments of time. As we have already noted, knowledge is an inverse pyramid (Isaiah 28:9-10; cf. chart # 2). God's revelation given to man from Adam to Moses covered a period of 2500 years with God using Moses to record it. From the first human author to the last covered a period of about 1600 years, from the 15th century B.C. to ca. 97 A.D. with forty human writers. It is essential for us to understand that an important purpose of each writer was to serve his own generation. This, alone, establishes the need for a dispensational study of the Bible.

The second reason for a dispensational study of the Bible is that the Bible clearly states that God has a program for the ages. Hebrews 1:1-2 states: *"God, who at sundry times and in divers manners spake in times past unto the fathers by the prophets, hath in these last days spoken unto us by his Son, whom he hath appointed heir of all things, by whom also he made the worlds…"*. The word translated "sundry" is *polumeros* which literally means "in many portions or variously as to time and agency." In that he said: *"Hath in these last days spoken"* relates to what has gone before, all of the various other times that God spoke through different men, indicating the progressive nature of God's revelation. He also stated: *"by whom also he made the worlds"* (aionos, the ages) or dispensations. Understand that the Greek word *kosmos* is the word used to signify the physical earth in the Bible (cf. Matthew 4:8; John 1:9, etc). Notice the interesting progression found in Acts 15:13-18. Verse fourteen speaks of the out-gathering of Gentiles (the church). Verse sixteen speaks of the ultimate re-gathering of Israel. And verse seventeen looks forward to the in-gathering of the world. This is dispensational language that, as it speaks of different actions in different time elements, points to the importance of a dispensational study.

It is important, also, for us to understand that dispensations are the only means of harmonizing all apparent contradictions that are generally related to different actions in different time frames, thus enabling us to better understand Scripture. Again, it is essential that the Bible be understood in the light of the time in which it was written. Understanding the context helps to keep us from developing a pretext, thus enabling us to find the truth that God is seeking to teach us.

The fourth reason the study of dispensations is important is because man can never be completely oriented to history apart from an understanding of the progressive dispensational rule of God. The Bible is and must be understood as the basic history book of this world. Thus history is to be understood in relation to biblical revelation, not the Bible interpreted by history. A study of dispensations gives us the key to this understanding.

BIBLICAL COVENANTS

As we continue, it is important that we see there is no contradiction between dispensations and covenants as some today teach. Just as dispensations are an integral part of the Bible, so are covenants of which there are eight. All of the biblical covenants were given in what we know as the Old Testament economy. Thus, when we find covenants mentioned in the New Testament, they always relate to the covenants found in the Old Testament.

There are two kinds of covenants found in the Bible. Some covenants recorded in the Bible are covenants made between men. One example is found in Malachi 2:14 which describes marriage as a covenant relationship. The second kind of covenant recorded in scripture is the covenant between God and man. The covenants of concern in this study are those between God and man. The Hebrew word translated "covenant" is *"berith"* which has the sense of the fettering or binding of the parties together. Covenants were God's way of establishing a working relationship with His creation.

Biblical covenants between God and man are easily identifiable as they are legal documents following a clear formula. First, we must understand that biblical covenants are always unilateral. In this case covenants are always an obligation imposed by a superior on an inferior. They are never formulated by God and man sitting down at a bargaining table to iron out an agreement as with management and labor. They are unilateral, always from God to man.

Second, Biblical covenants are either conditional or unconditional. The formula for a conditional covenant is when God states to those with whom He is making the covenant: "If you, I will." The most noted conditional covenant is the Mosaic Covenant. Read Deuteronomy chapter 28 and note the blessings that God promises to those who are obedient and the curses for those who are not. You may also recognize that the list of curses is much longer than the list of blessings. It is noteworthy here to see that blessings accrue because of obedience. They are never promised unconditionally, but are always the direct result of or reward for obedience.

The formula for an unconditional covenant is when God simply states: "I will." In this case, the keeping of the covenant conditions are totally God's responsibility. We will more fully develop this thought when we look at the specific covenants.

Of the eight covenants, only two are conditional: the Edenic and Mosaic Covenants. The other six covenants are all unconditional. The first three covenants relate to man in general, whereas the other five covenants relate more specifically to the Jew and the nation of Israel. However, the Abrahamic and New Covenants do have aspects that relate to both Jew and Gentile as we shall later see in this study. There are, however, aspects of each covenant that affect the covenants that follow. With each covenant there is a specific test of obedience. The result of how man faired in that test affects the covenants that follow. Also, promises given in the unconditional Covenants are eternal and become a part of each of the covenants that follow them. This will become important to our understanding of the relationship between the covenants and dispensations as we further develop this study.

It is also important for us to note that the specific emphasis of biblical covenants is on God's relationship to man, whereas the emphasis of dispensations is more on the time element. Because one emphasizes time and the other emphasizes man, there is a clear relationship between covenants and dispensations. Thus, in order to fully understand God's program for the ages we must understand both dispensations and covenants and their relationship to each other within God's Word. We will learn that they become the two banks of the river through which God's progressive revelation flows (cf. chart #2).

Why is it important for us in the church age to understand the role of covenants? Jesus Himself made the connection as He celebrated Passover with His disciples for the last time. When He took the cup He stated: *"For this is my blood of the new testament which is shed for many for the remission of sins."* (Matthew 26:28). The word translated "testament" is diatheke which could just as well be translated "covenant". The writer of Hebrews makes this clear in Hebrews 8:7-13; 10:1-14. Thus are Gentiles grafted into the true faith (cf. Romans 11:13-18) through the sacrifice of God's Lamb that instituted the New Covenant at Calvary.

Remember, the purpose of this study is to show the progressive flow of God's revelation, the umbilical cord from which all biblical truth emanates. As you develop this understanding it will help you to better grasp the flow of biblical revelation along with the flow of history enabling you to more fully appreciate what God is doing with His world today and to better understand all biblical truth and what God is planning to do in the future. As you come to recognize that all other truths emanate from this umbilical cord of truth the Word of God will come alive with understanding.

CHAPTER 2

FOUNDATIONS II

Understanding Biblical covenants and dispensations and their relationship to each other is foundational to grasping the truths of God's Word. Covenants and dispensations establish the operating conditions (time frame and relationships) for understanding the biblical spectrum. Thus, as we move forward with this study, we shall consider the biblical sources for both covenants and dispensations by which we shall begin to see the relationship between them. There are eight biblical covenants and seven biblical dispensations. First, we shall consider chronologically the covenants, their source and type.

THE COVENANTS

THE EDENIC COVENANT

The first covenant was made by God with Adam and Eve. This is the Edenic Covenant. It begins with man's creation and ends with the fall of man. The basic biblical passages covered are: Genesis 1:26-31 and Genesis 2:15-25. This is a conditional covenant based upon the test of obedience found in Genesis 2:16-17. Herein was blessing and cursing upon one's simple act of faithfulness to God determined by their obedience to God's command not to partake of a certain fruit in the garden. They could freely partake of all the other fruit. The covenant was canceled (broken) when Adam and Eve disobeyed.

THE ADAMIC COVENANT

The second covenant is the Adamic Covenant. After man's fall this covenant replaced the Edenic Covenant. As this covenant is unconditional, its major aspects extend to eternity. The covenant is stated in Genesis 3:14-21. This covenant is established after the fall with Adam and Eve. The essence of this covenant is the unconditional promise of a redeemer (cf. 3:15). At this point it is essential to make clear that all of the covenants that follow do not cancel the unconditional aspects of the previous covenant(s). The promise of a Redeemer is an unconditional promise, the fulfillment of which becomes a part of all further covenants.

THE NOAHIC COVENANT

The third covenant is the Noahic Covenant. This covenant is laid out for us in Genesis 9:1-18. As you read this foundational passage, note that God never uses the conditional word "if". So this is also an unconditional covenant. The essence of this covenant is two-fold: The establishment of capital punishment (Genesis 9:6) and the assurance that God would never again destroy the earth with a flood (Genesis 9:11). The time frame for this covenant is from after the worldwide flood and continues to earth's end.

THE ABRAHAMIC COVENANT

The fourth covenant is the Abrahamic Covenant. This covenant is also unconditional (Genesis 15:7-11, 17-18). It begins with the call of Abram and extends through eternity. The three basic elements of this covenant are: 1. The promise of a land; 2. The promise of numerous descendents, a seed; 3. The promise of redemption, both national and universal. We will note later, when we look at these covenants more in depth, that the final three covenants are an expansion of the three basic elements of the Abrahamic Covenant (cf. chart #3). This covenant is basically stated in Genesis 12:1-3 and further explained in Genesis 13:14-17; 15: 1 -7; 17:1-8. As this covenant is so foundational to God's eternal program for the ages and to any true understanding of world history, it is absolutely essential that one fully understands it. We will discuss the importance of this covenant more in depth as we continue through this study.

THE MOSAIC COVENANT

The fifth covenant is the Mosaic Covenant. It extends from the giving of the law on Mount Sinai to the death of Christ on the cross at Calvary. This covenant was made specifically with Israel and is laid out in detail from Exodus 19:1 through Deuteronomy 28:65. This covenant is conditional. In Deuteronomy chapter 28 we find a list of the blessings for obedience and the curses that accrue for disobedience. Because most of this covenant relates specifically to Israel, there is little here that has a direct relationship to the non-Jewish world. To insist on applying the elements of this covenant to the non-Jewish world is to deliberately refuse to recognize the context of both time and relationships and to rebel against God's clearly-stated truth. However, as we study this covenant, we can learn a great deal about God and how He deals with His creation. But it must always be understood in the context of a conditional covenant which was made specifically with Israel and the Jewish people.

THE PALESTINIAN COVENANT

The sixth covenant is the Palestinian Covenant. It becomes effective after the Exodus and extends into eternity. This covenant is stated, among other places, in Deuteronomy 29:1 through 30:9. This covenant primarily deals with the unconditional land promise that God gave to Israel through the Abrahamic Covenant (cf. chart #3).

THE DAVIDIC COVENANT

The seventh covenant is the Davidic Covenant. It began with King David and extends to eternity because it is an unconditional covenant. The basic statement of this covenant is found in II Samuel 7:4-16. It more fully explains and expands the second unconditional promise of national blessing found in the Abrahamic Covenant. This covenant also relates most specifically to Israel and the Jewish people but has ramifications for future end time events as we shall see later (cf. chart #3).

THE NEW COVENANT

The final biblical covenant is the New Covenant. This covenant is instituted by Christ's death at Calvary and extends into eternity. Thus it is an unconditional covenant. The primary statement of this covenant is found in Jeremiah 31:31-34. It is further mentioned in Deuteronomy 30:6; Isaiah 61:8-9; Ezekiel 37:36. It is through this covenant, as we shall discuss more fully later in this study, that the Gentiles are grafted into the true biblical faith (cf. Romans 11:13-21; Matthew 26:26 -29; Hebrews 7:18-19; 8:7-13; 10:9) as was God's intent from the beginning.

THE DISPENSATIONS

At this point in our study we are only interested, as was the case with the covenants, in identifying the dispensations and their time frame, so that we may begin to understand how biblical covenants and dispensations relate to one another. Dispensations are much simpler, as the emphasis of each dispensation is upon how God governs the world and man's responsibility during the extent of the dispensation. Both of these elements change with each dispensation. The emphasis is on time. There are seven dispensations clearly established in God's Word.

INNOCENCE

The first dispensation is the dispensation of Innocence. This dispensation begins with the creation of man and concludes with Divine judgment after man's fall. The scripture covered is Genesis 1:26 to Genesis 3:24.

CONSCIENCE

The second dispensation is the dispensation of Conscience. It begins after man's judgment following the fall and continues through the flood of Noah's day. The scripture covered by this dispensation is from Genesis 4:1 to Genesis 8:13.

HUMAN GOVERNMENT

The third dispensation is the dispensation of Human Government. This dispensation begins after the flood and continues through the Tower of Babel. It begins with Genesis 8:15 and concludes with Genesis 11:9.

PROMISE

The fourth dispensation is the dispensation of Promise. It begins with the call of Abram and concludes with Moses receiving the law at Sinai. The scripture covered is from Genesis 11:10 to Exodus 18:27.

LAW

The fifth dispensation is the dispensation of the law. It begins with Moses at Sinai and concludes with Christ's death on Calvary. It extends from Exodus 19:1 to John 21:25 (cf. Matthew 26:26-29).

GRACE

The sixth dispensation is the dispensation of Grace. This dispensation begins immediately after Calvary and concludes with the judgments immediately following Christ's second coming. Scripturally it covers the time from the resurrection accounts to Revelation 19:21.

MILLENNIAL KINGDOM

The final dispensation is the dispensation of the Kingdom. Revelation 20:1-15 gives us the biblical record of this dispensation. It begins with Christ's reign on David's throne and extends one thousand years concluding with the Great White Throne Judgment.

A DISPENSATIONAL PERSPECTIVE

There are many ways to look at dispensations. However, as we move forward and expand this study, we will consider eight specific ingredients that will help us to develop a good perspective of each dispensation.

1. The age in general.
2. The extent of the period (beginning and ending).
3. The general scripture portions (where it begins to where a new dispensation is established).
4. The characteristics or state of man during the course of the dispensation.
5. The special responsibility of man (the divine test).
6. The failure of man under the test.
7. The resulting divine judgment
8. The gracious intervention of God.

We will also note that with each dispensation God deals with a very specific excuse that could be offered by man as to why he (man) failed. By the time history as we know it ends God will have answered every excuse of man so that when man stands before the Great White Throne he will have no excuses left to offer. Thus, in the final chapter of history God will be seen as both just and benevolent for having provided man with everything he needed by His grace to be all that God intended him to be.

CHAPTER 3

THE EDENIC COVENANT AND THE DISPENSATION OF INNOCENCE

THE EDENIC COVENANT

The Edenic Covenant and the dispensation of Innocence cover the same period of time in man's history. Both begin with man's creation and end with man's expulsion from the Garden of Eden. This was the covenant God established with Adam when He placed him in the Garden. After creating the world and all that is in it, God gave Adam and his wife several responsibilities (cf. Genesis 1:28). First, they were instructed to *"be fruitful and multiply and replenish the earth and subdue it."* The Hebrew word translated "replenish" is mala and simply means "to fill." So their first work was to propagate. Their second responsibility was to *"subdue it* (the earth) *and have dominion over the fish of the sea and over the foul of the air, and over every living thing that moveth upon the earth."* God gave to Adam dominion over the animal world. It was God's intention that Adam be sovereign over the world. According to Genesis 2:15 Adam was to *"till the garden and keep it."* It is interesting to note that even in a perfect world the land needed to be cultivated. Thus Adam and Eve were able to enjoy the fruit of their labor. Further, God told Adam and Eve that they could partake of the fruit of every tree except of the tree of the knowledge of good and evil (cf. Genesis 2:16-17). Here was the test of obedience. He informed them that if they ate of the forbidden fruit they would surely die. Thus the maintenance of this covenant was a prerequisite upon their obedience not to eat of the forbidden fruit. The fact that the covenant was annulled when they disobeyed is illustrated by the broken fellowship between God and man. (cf. Genesis 3:8-11). The result of death is separation. In this case that separation was two-fold. Adam and Eve died spiritually (separated from their Creator) the moment they disobeyed. But they also began to die physically. The fact that man began to die physically the moment that he disobeyed is made clear in Genesis 3:17-19. By the time we get into Genesis chapter four physical death is a very clear reality. It is clear that when one looks at the primitive roots of the Hebrew word for death, they spring from the very beginnings of speech. As, according to God's promise, man did immediately die spiritually, it only follows that His promise of physical death also became a reality. Thus we see that this covenant was conditional. Its beginning and ending are an historical fact.

There are some who do not see this as a covenant as the word "covenant" is never used nor do we find the phrase "I will" which is considered an integral part of the covenant formula. However, the "if you-I will" formula is expressed in the test of obedience. If man eats of the forbidden fruit the result is death. If he is obedient to the command the blessings would continue. That is clearly the teaching of the text. This first chapter in the history of man involves a responsibility and an ethical test, both essential elements in a covenant. The other important issue here is that it is only God who establishes the conditions of this new relationship which is, indeed, the case here.

"And the LORD God commanded the man, saying, Of every tree of the garden thou mayest freely eat: But of the tree of the knowledge of good and evil, thou shalt not eat of it: for in the day that thou eatest thereof thou shalt surely die." (Genesis 2:16, 17). Herein was both blessing and cursing based upon one's simple faithfulness to God determined by their obedience to God's command not to partake of a certain fruit. All of the other fruit they could freely partake. As the maintenance of the covenant was determined by Adam's obedience this covenant is conditional. Thus the covenant was broken when Adam and Eve disobeyed and partook of the forbidden fruit. Remember, the simple definition of death is separation. Physical death is the separation of the soul and spirit from the body, whereas, spiritual death is man being separated from God. This is the loss of man's ability to fellowship with God. Adam and Eve immediately died spiritually as is seen in

Genesis 3:8-11. Also, the process of physical death was begun the moment they ate of the forbidden fruit. It was Paul who wrote that *"The wages of sin is death; but the gift of God is eternal life."* Sin brought death into the world. The further result of their rebellion was their expulsion from the garden.

There is an interesting side truth here that is often missed. It is found in God's reason for removing Adam and Eve from the garden. Notice God's reason stated in Genesis 3:22. *"Now, lest he put forth his hand, and take also of the tree of life, and eat, and live forever...."*. We may note two things. They obviously had not eaten of the fruit from the tree of life. Had they done so they would have lived forever in their now sinful rebellious state. Second, this was an act of God's grace to keep them from such an awful fate.

THE DISPENSATION OF INNOCENCE

The Dispensation of Innocence is also based upon the Edenic Covenant test. This is the age of Adam. The period extends from the creation of man to his fall and expulsion from the Garden of Eden. The biblical passages covered are from Genesis 1:26 to 3:24. Man's state was ideal. Upon his creation God placed man in a beautiful garden where his environment was perfect (Genesis 2:8). He had an innocent nature as he knew not sin (Genesis 2:17, 25). All of his temporal needs were freely supplied (cf. Genesis 1:29; 2:9, 16). Man had everything, lacking nothing. He was given great mental prowess as seen in his ability to name every living creature that God made (Genesis 2:19, 20, 23). God even gave to Adam a companion (Genesis 2:18) to be his helper and mate, providing the divine basis for marriage (Genesis 2:24).

Man also had God-given work to constructively employ his time (Genesis 1:28; 2: 15). As the supreme act of God's creation (created in God's own image), man was further given dominion over all the creatures that God had created and they were commanded to multiply, replenish and subdue the earth (Genesis 1:26 -28). This was an awesome responsibility, but God had given to man everything he needed to accomplish this great work.

Man enjoyed a personal relationship with God (Genesis 3:8). God walked in the earth that He might fellowship with His creation. Man's every need was met. He could walk with God and enjoy an intimate relationship with Him. The environment was perfect. He was given constructive work to do. Everything was perfect.

But there was a test, a test of obedience. This was necessary for God and man to truly have fellowship with one another. Fellowship is based upon the free choice of both parties involving trust. So God had to create a circumstance whereby man could make that free choice involving an act of obedience. All man had to do was refuse to eat of the fruit that God forbad him to eat. They were asked to believe that God had their best interest at heart. They were to recognize God's headship and governmental authority in the earth (Genesis 2:16-17). This became the very issue upon which the serpent attacked Eve, a mental, psychological seduction, (cf. Genesis 3:4-5). This is still the basis upon which Satan seeks to attack us today.

But not even innocence in this perfect environment was enough to keep man from disobeying God. The temptation (test) was to have what God forbad (Genesis 3:5). To know what God had not revealed and to be what God had not purposed for man to be thus created the temptation to act independently of God. The temptation was an appeal to the lust of the flesh, the lust of the eyes, and the pride of life. And man fell!

There is an interesting sidelight here. The serpent attacked Eve and, being beguiled, she fell. It was Eve who then gave to Adam the forbidden fruit. Let us be reminded that God had established Adam as the head of the household. Humanly speaking, the buck stopped at Adam's desk. Even after his wife had eaten, he did not have to eat of the forbidden fruit. He had a choice. It was a choice to have fellowship either with God, his Creator, or with his wife. If Adam chose not to eat of the fruit, he would lose his relationship with Eve but maintain his relationship with God. If he chose to eat of the forbidden fruit, he understood that he could maintain his relationship with Eve but lose his relationship with God. He chose the latter. So his was a clear and deliberate choice to follow Eve in the rebellion. Thus it was established that the sin nature would be passed down through the male (Romans 5:12) and not through the female establishing the necessity of a Virgin Birth (cf. Genesis 3:15) to assure a perfect redemptive sacrifice.

Note the Divine judgment as recorded in Genesis 3:7, 22-24. The implication in this text is that if man had not sinned, he and his posterity would have grown in knowledge and life before God. It would have been ever upward and onward. Satan today still tries to convince us that he can get it for us quicker and better. So, as God intended His revelation to man to be progressive, the tragedy is that man missed the fact that God would have ultimately shared a complete revelation with him as he was able to deal righteously with that revelation.

By Adam's failure, death and sin came into the world, upon him and all of his posterity (Genesis 3:7.17; Romans 7:15-25). Thus man died immediately. The fellowship Adam had with God was broken as illustrated by the fact that they hid themselves from God (cf. Genesis 3:8). Remember, physical death is the separation of the soul and spirit from the body. Spiritual death is the separation of the soul and spirit of man from God.

But let us also note God's gracious intervention. In judgment and wrath God remembered mercy (Habakkuk 3:2). Otherwise, in Adam the race would have been annihilated (*For the wages of sin is death.* Romans 6:23a). God gave man another opportunity to perform righteously under other conditions if, indeed, such were possible. He gave Adam and Eve the promise of a Redeemer (Genesis 3:15). God also gave them a gracious covering, a coat, whereas Adam made only an apron (Genesis 3:2, 21). God also graciously expelled them from the garden so that man would not partake of the tree of life creating the situation of man living on earth forever in his now sinful and rebellious state, which would have necessitated man's destruction (Genesis 3:22-24).

One great truth to be learned here is that through the dispensations God is answering every possible excuse that man can offer for his failures so that when he (man) stands before God to be judged, man will be without excuse. Here man had a perfect life with everything that he needed, including the best of all circumstances. Yet he still failed.

CHAPTER 4

THE ADAMIC COVENANT AND THE DISPENSATION OF CONSCIENCE

The Edenic Covenant and the Dispensation of Innocence ended in disaster, bringing upon man God's judgment. This was followed by His gracious intervention leading to the next phase of man's history in God's plan. This brings us to a consideration of God's covenant with Adam and the Dispensation of Conscience.

THE ADAMIC COVENANT

We have little biblical material with which to deal in relation to the first three covenants. Yet, understanding these early covenants is important if we are to grasp the flow of God's revelation of truth. These early covenants are the foundation pieces upon which God builds. The Edenic Covenant deals with creation and the initial relationship between God and man. The Adamic Covenant deals with man's fall into sin and God's response. All of this establishes the foundation for the rest of God's revelation of truth to man.

First, it is important to understand that this covenant is unconditional. Therefore, the divine promise given in this covenant follows through to eternity. Before we look at the promise, we must look at the results of the rebellion.

As a result of Adam's rebellion God responded with a fourfold curse. First, He cursed the serpent who was Satan's instrument to tempt Eve. God said: *"Because thou hast done this, thou art cursed above all cattle, and above every beast of the field; upon thy belly shalt thou go, and dust shalt thou eat all the days of thy life."* (Genesis 3:14). God cursed the serpent to become vile and a reproach in the eyes of man. He forever would crawl in the dust and be caused to eat what he would not, the dust of the earth.

God goes on to state: *"And I will put enmity between thee and the woman, and between thy seed and her seed; it shall bruise thy head, and thou shalt bruise his heel"* (Genesis 3:15). Here in this one verse is established the conflict between good and evil; between God and Satan; between Grace and corruption in the heart of man. Also here we have the promise of a Redeemer with the assurance that through the Redeemer righteousness will win in the end. We also see the heart of God's Grace (undeserved favor) in the promise of a deliverer. It is clear in Genesis 4:1 that Eve understood this promise as she thought that Cain would be that redeemer.

This verse also establishes the necessity of the virgin birth of the Messiah-Redeemer. Two things are important to remember. God made Adam responsible to Him. When Eve was beguiled (cf. Genesis 3:13), she offered the forbidden fruit to Adam who willfully chose to partake. Adam had a choice. He could refuse to eat in obedience to God and thus maintain his relationship with God or eat of the fruit and maintain his relationship with Eve. Thus did Paul write speaking of Adam: *"Wherefore as by one man sin entered into the world, and death by sin; and so death passed upon all men, for that all have sinned."* (Romans 5:12). Paul reaffirms this truth in I Corinthians 15:21-22. In I Timothy 2:13-14 this truth is again stated with one further bit of information: *"And Adam was not deceived."* Thus is the sin nature passed through the male necessitating the virgin birth.

Also, when Adam and Eve were created, they were created perfect, without sin. They were placed into a perfect relationship with God, the fellowship of which was broken by man's sin. The broken fellowship necessitated a means whereby the relationship with God could be re-established so that man again could fellowship with God and God with man. As God cannot tolerate sin, sin had to be paid for necessitating some means of redemption that was acceptable to God. The genesis of that plan was laid out as God dealt with the serpent in that He stated that the woman's seed would bruise the serpent's head; that is, ultimately put him to death.

The result of the fall is that God cursed the woman (Genesis 3:16). Sin brought sorrow into the world. If there had been no sin, man would not have known sorrow. The woman is told that her sorrow in childbearing would be greatly increased. How great is a mother's sorrow when her children rebel against both parental authority and God's authority as well.

When God created Eve, it was God's intent to give Adam a helper (Genesis 2:21-24). As such they were to function as one. God, from the beginning in creating Adam first and Eve out of him, held Adam accountable. As her desire was always to be a helper and encourager to her husband, Adam always had authority over his wife. But her subjection was intended to be willing. Because of the entrance of sin, God now required it (Genesis 3:16).

It is an interesting fact that by woman came sin. But by woman came also the Saviour. In Satan's seed will come the antichrist. In the woman's seed came the Saviour, Christ Jesus. In these two persons, all prophecy ultimately converges as we shall later see.

As a result of the fall of Adam, God also cursed the ground. *"Cursed is the ground for thy sake; in sorrow shalt thou eat of it all the days of thy life; thorns and thistles shall it bring forth to thee; and thou shalt eat the herb of the field.* (Genesis 3:17-18).

Labor, which was to be a blessing, now becomes the source of sorrow and anguish for man. *"In the sweat of thy face shalt thou eat bread."* Then God confirms the earlier stated result of sin (Genesis 2:16-17) as now a fact (*For out of it wast thou taken; for dust thou art, and unto dust shalt thou return"*). Spiritual death occurred immediately upon their eating of the forbidden fruit. Here God confirms the entrance of physical death into the world scene.

God confirms this new covenant with a blood sacrifice in the killing of animals to provide for Adam and Eve an effective covering of their bodies. This symbolized His redemptive plan enabling man to be re-established in his relationship with his Creator, thus making possible for man to continue to have fellowship with God. However, the gift of eternal life was now withheld, as God drove man from the garden so that they could not eat of the fruit of the tree of life. We shall later see that this gift is re-instated through the sacrifice of God's Lamb, His Son, on Calvary for all who will receive it.

It is with this covenant that God provides salvation from sin on the basis of faith in a covering sacrifice that was intended by God to point to the sacrifice of His perfect Lamb. Thus salvation must, from the very beginning, be received, not in an act of man, but by faith in God's promised ultimate redemption through the perfect sacrifice that He would one day provide. This covenant now becomes the pattern of man's life, resulting in his expulsion from the Garden of Eden.

THE DISPENSATION OF CONSCIENCE

Let us now turn our attention to the Dispensation of Conscience which parallels the Adamic Covenant. The age in general was that of Cain and his immediate descendents. The time period extends from the fall of man to the flood. This period is covered in the Bible beginning with Genesis 4:1 and concludes with Genesis 8:19.

As this dispensation begins, man is no longer innocent. He now knows the difference between good and evil. This brought about the development of a conscience, which was not a part of God's original endowment. Man's conscience came as a result of sin.

Man lost all the blessed conditions of his previous state. He was expelled from the garden. He had to win his food by the sweat of his brow (cf. Genesis 3:17-19). His mental faculties were dulled and perverted (cf. Genesis 6:5). His work was no longer a pleasure, but became arduous (Genesis 4:11-15). He

25

began to choose "fair" wives regardless of God's will (cf. Genesis 4:19; 6: 2).

However, Seth called upon God (cf. Genesis 4:25 -26). The "Sons of God" of Genesis 6:1-2 refer to the descendents of Seth who trusted in the Lord but whose children inter-married with women descended from Cain. Thus, against God's plan for man, the marriage union began to be between the godly and the ungodly families of men. By marrying multiple wives, they also broke God's clear command that marriage was to be between one man and one woman (cf. Genesis 2:24).

The principle of the blood sacrifice for sin was clearly established in Genesis 3:22-24. In Genesis chapter four the text implies that Cain and Abel were taught the necessity of a blood sacrifice in order to approach God, and that probably there was a regular place and time for that sacrifice to be offered. We need to note that Cain was not an atheist. He believed in God, but was angry that he could not worship Him as his own mind dictated. But the first fruit of his labor was not enough, because God demanded a blood sacrifice. Again we see the establishment of the principle that salvation is not of works, but by faith in the shed blood of the innocent victim.

Man was again forewarned of judgment by Noah's preaching (cf. II Peter 2:5) as they sought not God (cf. Genesis 6:5-7). It is important here to note that when God created man, man was created to have fellowship with God. In the perfectness of the Garden of Eden, where there was no sin, that fellowship existed unhindered. But when man sinned, all of that changed. Fellowship was lost. Man's sin had to be dealt with in order for there to again be fellowship between God and man. God removed their sin guilt through a blood sacrifice enabling Him to again have fellowship with man. This is redemption. But fellowship with God is still dependent upon man not sinning. In all of the economies prior to the cross God provided both redemption and forgiveness as man faithfully offered the required sacrifice to cover his continued sinning. God's provision of redemption is seen in the animals killed to provide for Adam and Eve a covering (Genesis 3:21). This re-established the fellowship between God and man. However, as man continued to sin, fellowship was broken. Thus God required man to offer blood sacrifices to cover those sins, so that the fellowship lost because of man's sinning could be re-established. God bought man back from the market of sin. Now, for man to maintain his fellowship with God, man had to offer the required sacrifice to cover his sins. As we shall later see as all of this develops, both the atonement sacrifice and the sin sacrifices were intended by God to point man to the one sacrifice that God Himself had promised (the Redeemer, Genesis 3:15). So it is important for us to understand that, from the beginning, God made a difference between salvation (relationship) and fellowship.

In this dispensation man's special responsibility was, with the guidance of conscience, to do good and to approach God by means of a sacrifice as taught them by the example of the victim, which provided the coats of skin. However, conscience was not enough to keep man from sinning against God (cf. Genesis 6:5). Man was indifferent to his conscience and thereby silenced and seared it. So, though the long suffering of God waited in the days of Noah (I Peter 3:20), God changed His method of dealing with man and sent the flood by which He destroyed all but eight souls.

Nevertheless God did not make a full end of man. Noah found favor in the eyes of God. Again, God intervened and saved mankind through Noah who, by faith in God's Word, prepared an ark to the saving of his household (Hebrews 11:7), preparing the way for God's next step of His plan for mankind and the ages.

Man's excuse that God deals with here is: "If I had been given understanding of right and wrong and some motivation to choose right, I would not have failed." God dealt with the sin problem. He gave man a conscience that warned man of sin. He warned man of the consequences of his sin. But none of this hindered man from doing what he set his mind to do. Man again failed. So we see the parallel between the Adamic Covenant and the Dispensation of Conscience.

CHAPTER 5

THE NOAHIC COVENANT AND THE DISPENSATION OF HUMAN GOVERNMENT

Again man failed God's test. And again God both judged and showed grace giving to mankind yet another opportunity for man to prove himself. As with the previous tests, this test involved both a divine covenant and a dispensation. It is important to note that, even though the covenant is unconditional, there is always a test for man to either pass or fail.

THE NOAHIC COVENANT

First, it is important to understand that this is an unconditional covenant. Five times God states: *I will* (Genesis 8:21; 9:11, 15, 16). Nowhere does God say to Noah *If you*. By describing this as an "everlasting" covenant God clearly described this covenant as unconditional.

God talked with Noah about this covenant before the flood (Gen. 6:18), but did not actually establish it with him until after the flood (cf. Genesis 9:11). This covenant included a restatement of responsibilities given to Adam. In Genesis 9:1 God said to Noah: *"Be fruitful and multiply, and replenish the earth."* In Genesis 9:2 God transferred to Noah the same dominion over the earth that He had given to Adam resulting in the animal world fearing man.

With this covenant God uniquely established two new things. First, with the authorization of capital punishment, God established human government (cf. Genesis 9:5-6). It was to be the responsibility of human government to establish laws with clear penalties, including capital punishment, to deter man from his wicked ways. Second, God promised never again to destroy the earth with a worldwide flood (Genesis 9:12-15). He promised the rainbow as a sign of His faithfulness to keep this promise forever.

Noah failed as is seen in Genesis 9:21-29. Though God's Grace persisted, Genesis 10 records the moral demise of the race over the next 900 plus years ending in God's judgment at the tower of Babel.

THE DISPENSATION OF HUMAN GOVERNMENT

The dispensation of Human Government parallels the Noahic Covenant. So this dispensation generally covers the age of Noah. It extends from the flood to the Tower of Babel. The scripture covered is from Genesis 8:15 to Genesis 11:9. This period is characterized by the development of law and government (Genesis 9:5-6). Man, with practical knowledge of his failure under conscience, is now made responsible to impose law, order and government upon his fellowman. This responsibility is seen in the command to take human life (Genesis 9:6). The ultimate punishment for one who murders another was to be the loss of their life. As this is an unconditional covenant it is still God's command for today.

In this command capital punishment was established as the highest function of human government. The reason for the establishment of capital punishment by God was to emphasize that man was made in God's image thus establishing the sacredness of life. The principle established is that, if a man murder another human being, his life is to be taken from him as he has dishonored the very image of God. If man abuses this responsibility then, he, too, was to be held accountable.

Man's failure under this dispensation is recorded in Genesis 11:1-4. Chapter ten mentions seventy nations. But, unfortunately, these nations did not rule for God, even though they were organized and developed. They continued to cultivate fellowship with sinful man rather than with God. Having gathered in the plains of Shinar, they got the idea of human brotherhood and sought to make a name for themselves choosing their own gods (cf. Romans 1). This became a period of idolatry and moral degradation brought about by the fact of man's turning away from God.

God's judgment is recorded in Genesis 11:5-9. Man, having lost fellowship with God, thought to have strength in union with other men. Brotherhood became the driving force. So God confounded their speech and caused them to scatter over the earth as He had first commanded them to do. Genesis 10:32 tells how God scattered them. After this, according to Daniel 3:7, men were brought back together in order to defy the true God with the use of the universal language of music.

Again, Grace intervened. God does not make a complete end of man but gives him yet another opportunity to do that which is right. God chooses Abram. And through him a nation was to be established in contrast with all other nations of the world. God's purpose in this was to maintain the possibility of redeeming mankind. The nation of Israel was established to be God's showpiece of His Grace for all the nations of the world to see.

As we move on to the next test it needs to be understood that God never chooses anyone for blessings. He chooses men for service. Blessings are the bi-product of faithful service. That was to be the whole point of choosing Israel, as we shall see.

CHAPTER 6

THE ABRAHAMIC COVENANT AND THE DISPENSATION OF PROMISE

We have learned to this point that all divine truth begins with three great foundational truths found in the first three chapters of Genesis. All biblical truth develops from these three foundational truths clearly demonstrating that God's revelation of truth is progressive. Since God's revelation of truth is progressive, we have seen that it develops between biblical dispensations and covenants (cf. chart #2). We have further noted that biblical covenants and dispensations are compatible and not contradictory, because biblical covenants emphasize the relationship between God and man, whereas dispensations emphasize the time frame (cf. chart #1).

Each covenant/dispensation embodies a test of man's faith. With each failure on the part of man, God intervenes with Grace as He maintains His program for the ultimate redemption of His Creation. Now, for the first time since Adam, God focuses His redemptive program on one man, Abram.

The importance of understanding the Abrahamic Covenant cannot be underestimated in developing a sound understanding of God's progressive revelation of scripture. Arthur Pink, in describing the literary organization of Genesis, stated: "Its literary structure is true to its title for the whole of its contents center around three beginnings. First, there is the beginning of the human race in Adam; second, there is the new beginning on the post-diluvian earth in Noah and his sons; third, there is the beginning of the chosen nation in Abram."ii He further went on to say: "This Divine preface is given to explain that which is made known in all that follows."iii

The covenant God makes with Abram becomes the foundation for all of the following covenants in the sense that, in this covenant is the seed for all of the covenants that are to follow. As we progress through this study, we will note that the covenants that follow each take one aspect of the Abrahamic Covenant and more fully develop that special aspect (cf. chart #3). As this covenant establishes the necessary foundation for understanding the rest of the Bible and God's program for the ages, it is important that we clearly understand it.

THE ABRAHAMIC COVENANT
CONDITIONAL OR UNCONDITIONAL?

Since there is a difference of opinion as to whether the Abrahamic Covenant is conditional or unconditional, we must resolve this issue before we can consider its value and importance to the rest of our study. Generally, those who consider this covenant to be conditional hold to the theological framework of Replacement Theology. In order for them to teach that the Church has replaced Israel in God's program, they must teach that this covenant is conditional. If it is considered as unconditional, God confirms His eternal relationship with Israel and the Jewish people as His uniquely chosen people. The issue is not what theologians teach, but what God's word, the Bible, clearly teaches.

Those who teach that this covenant is conditional primarily base their claim on the fact that God said: *"Get thee out of thy country, and from thy kindred, and from thy father's house, unto a land that I will show thee* (Genesis 12:1). Since they view this statement as establishing the condition for implementation, they state that the covenant could only be operational "if" Abram was obedient to this "command" from God. As there is no question regarding the fact this covenant became operational, was Abram obedient to it?

If this statement establishes the conditions for implementation, what were the conditions stated? Those who see this statement as conditional must admit that there are three conditions stated. The first condition is *"Get thee out of thy country."* Abram was still living in Mesopotamia when God's call came to him, according to Acts 7:1-4. It is interesting that it was Abram's father who brought him from Ur to Haran along with Lot, Abram's nephew. They did not leave Haran until after Terah, Abram's father, had died. Abram certainly was partially obedient to this command as is so stated in Genesis 12:4. *"And so Abram departed, as the LORD had spoken unto him."* However, they stopped for several years in Haran, not going directly to the land that God promised him. Notice that the Bible states that they "dwelt there" (Genesis 11:31), indicating that they were there for an extended period of time.

The second condition was *"from thy kindred, and from thy father's house"*. He was called to separate himself from his father's idolatrous house and all of his relatives. But Abram did not do this. He went as far as Haran with his father and remained there until his father was dead. After Abram's father died notice what God's Word states: *"So Abram departed as the LORD had spoken unto him; and Lot went with him."* (Genesis 12:4). According to verse five they (Abram, Sarai, and Lot) left from Haran and *"they went forth to go into the land of Canaan; and into the land of Canaan they came."* So it becomes clear that Abram was not at all obedient to the second aspect of God's directions. He did not separate either from his father's house or from his kindred.

The third condition stated in the command was that Abram was to go into the land of Canaan as God had directed him. This he did. This was the only part of God's instructions to which Abram was totally obedient. Thus, if this statement lays out conditions for the inception of this covenant, the covenant never would have been instituted as two of the three conditions were not met.

The biblical evidence does not support the premise that the covenant God made with Abram was conditional. However, the language of the covenant does clearly show it to be unconditional. Four times in the three verses that lay out the promises of the covenant God said: "I will." There is not one time in this covenant statement where it is stated that God said "If you." The language of the covenant shows it to be an unconditional covenant.

The ultimate proof that this covenant is unconditional is found in Genesis 15 where God rehearses the covenant with Abram. In verses 7 to 17 God instructs Abram to kill some animals and birds, divide them in half, and put half on one side and half opposite them with enough space between for one to walk between them. This was the tradition when two people were entering into an agreement (covenant) in Abram's day (cf. Jeremiah 34:18). The parties of the covenant were then to walk between the animal parts indicating: "so do to me as has been done to these animals if I do not keep my part of the covenant agreement." When it came time to confirm the agreement, God caused a sleep to fall upon Abram (cf. Genesis 15:12) so that only God passed between the parts declaring this covenant to be unconditional. All of the responsibility for its fulfillment was taken by God. There is no question that this covenant is unconditional according to God's Word.

For those who desire a more complete discussion of the other scriptures used by some who support the idea that this covenant is conditional, see Dr. Renald Showers' book, THERE REALLY IS A DIFFERENCE, pages 60 to 68. Answering the objections of those who believe this covenant to be conditional, Dr. Showers gives ten reasons supported by the biblical text that clearly demonstrate this covenant to be unconditional.

THREE COVENANT PROMISES

God gave to Abram and to his posterity three unconditional promises. The first was a promise of national blessing (Genesis 12:1). This was a promise of a national land. So the Jewish people, the descendents of Abraham through Isaac and Jacob have a divine deed to their land. It is of interest as one studies the history of the Jewish people that God's blessings upon them are specifically related to their presence in the land He gave to them. This promise is more fully expanded, as we shall later see, in the Palestinian Covenant.

The second unconditional promise of this covenant is found in Genesis 12:2 and is a promise of numerous descendents to form a great nation. Abram was promised posterity (seed) without number and that through this seed, the whole world would be blessed. Both aspects of this promise already are fulfilled to date. The world certainly has been much blessed by, among other things, the music, agricultural, electronic, scientific and medical innovations that have come from Abram's seed down through the centuries. This promise is more fully expanded and expounded by the Davidic Covenant.

The third promise given found in Genesis 12:3 is a promise of universal blessing through Abram's seed. *"In thee shall all families of the earth be blessed."* This is a promise of redemption, both national and universal. Paul recognized this and so stated it to the Galatian Church. He wrote: *"Now to Abraham and his seed were the promises made. He saith not, And to seeds, as of many; but as of one, And to thy seed, which is Christ."* (Galatians 3:16). Indeed, the world has been blessed by the coming of the Messiah/Redeemer born of the seed of David who was of the seed of Abram. Through faith in the Messiah/Redeemer (Jesus, the Christ) alone is one saved from the just penalty of his sin, whether that one is Jewish or Gentile, fulfilling this great unconditional promise given to Abram of both national and universal blessing. This promise is more fully explained by the New Covenant, as we shall later learn.

Before we move on, it is important that we understand that this promise also incorporates a warning: *"I will bless them that bless thee, and curse him that curseth thee."* This is a warning to all who would, in any way, mistreat Abram's seed through Isaac and Jacob. This is a promise that God will protect the instrument through which He plans to bless the world: Israel (the Jewish people). History, through the centuries, has shown that those who treat Israel and the Jew well are blessed and that those who do not are cursed. For a good example, study the history of the British Empire. It was once said of them that the sun never sets on the British Empire. But after they reneged on their promise to implement the Balfour Declaration the empire disintegrated. Another good example to study is Germany.

Thus this covenant embodies three very specific promises: the promise of a land, the promise of a seed, and the promise of national and universal blessings. We may note that, in this covenant, certain individual promises were given to Abram; certain national promises respecting the nation of Israel, of which he was the father, were given to him; and certain universal blessings were given him that were to encompass all nations and peoples (cf. chart #3).

These covenant promises were passed down by God's direction to Isaac and Jacob, thus eliminating both Ishmael (cf. Genesis 21:12) and Esau. Regarding Esau, God renewed the covenant with Jacob, not Esau (cf. Genesis 28:10-15).

As we shall later see in this study, this covenant becomes the foundation of the rest of God's program for the Ages. As an unconditional covenant, its promises extend to eternity.

THE DISPENSATION OF PROMISE

The Dispensation of promise parallels the Abrahamic Covenant. The age is that of Abraham. The time frame for this dispensation extends from Abraham to Moses. It begins with Genesis 12 and concludes with Exodus 18:27. Man, in this dispensation, became the recipient of wonderful, gracious, and unconditional promises of Jehovah's purpose respecting Abraham and his seed.

Up to this point the dispensations included all mankind in their regulations. This dispensation was elective in that God chose out one man, Abram and his descendents to make a representative test with them. The test was whether great material, social and spiritual promises with their prospects would cause Abraham and his descendents to believe and faithfully serve Jehovah. The responsibility of Abraham and his descendents was to remain obediently in the land into which God had called him. They were to remain in faith in the place of promised blessing and continue separate from the nations around them. It is interesting to note that between Genesis 12:1 and Genesis 25:8 there is not one single "if" by which God conditioned His blessings to Abraham.

Though everything they could need and beyond was promised them, they still failed. Abraham, in a lack of faith, went down into Egypt (Genesis 12:10). When Sarai had no children and was past the age of childbearing Abram tried to help God by raising up seed through his Egyptian servant (Genesis 16:1-6). This act still has repercussions on his seed through Isaac, the promised son, to this very day. In relation to the issue of the Divine destruction of Sodom and Gomorrah, he apparently did not trust God to do the right thing (Genesis 18:16-33). Isaac failed because of a lack of faith in God's promises (Genesis 26:6-7). Jacob, too, failed in trusting God (Genesis 28:13-15, 20-22). After his name was changed from Jacob to Israel (Genesis 32:28), he again failed by choosing to go down to Egypt to permanently stay during a famine because his son, whom he thought was dead, was alive and living in Egypt. Notice the play on words. In Genesis 46:1 we are told that he took *"all that he had"*. This does not sound like someone just going for a visit. They got to Beersheba and there Israel decided that he should have checked with God (cf. Genesis 46:1b). *"And God spoke unto Israel in the visions of the night, and said, Jacob, Jacob."* (Genesis 46:2). God once again calls him "Suplanter, Suplanter" instead of "God shall rule" (Israel). It is clear that Israel (Jacob) had already made up his mind what he would do. Here we see God's permissive will.

The descent into Egypt was a judgment and punishment, as well as a failure. However, through it God worked out His sublime will and purpose. For Israel and his seed, they experienced sorrow, slavery and threatened extinction as a result of this decision. For Israel, the seed of Abram, the experience was exceedingly bitter.

If the Abrahamic Covenant is unconditional, and it is, then God was committed to the survival of Abram's seed through Isaac and Jacob. Though the blessings were lost, the promises remained sure. Egypt's bounty was not necessary. God would have kept them if they had just remained in the land. But, by God's grace, Israel was preserved in the furnace of Egypt. In time, Moses, a deliverer, was provided (cf. Exodus 3:6-10). Passover protection was provided for the guilty (Exodus 12). Redemption was made available through the blood of an innocent animal (*"When I see the blood I will pass over you"* (Exodus 12:13, 23). Here we see again the "exchange of life" principle that was established by God way back in Genesis 3:22. God's divine power wrought their deliverance. Egypt, the oppressor, was slain (cf. Exodus 14:28). God again began to miraculously supply both their material (Exodus 12:35-36) and physical needs (Exodus 15:23-37). Even victory over their new enemies was given them (cf. Exodus 17). Remember, every dispensation concludes with judgment and grace.

CONCLUSIONS

Again, we find no contradiction between covenants and dispensations. The covenant, in this case, lays out the promises. The dispensation lays out the test and the time frame. In this process God continues, by His grace, to extend the river of His truth, which can also be depicted as the umbilical cord of truth that extends from Genesis to Revelation from which all other truth radiates.

CHAPTER 7

THE MOSAIC, PALESTINIAN, DAVIDIC COVENANTS AND THE DISPENSATION OF THE LAW

As I was recently reading the Gospel accounts of the earthly ministry of Jesus, I was impressed as never before by the fact that when Jesus quoted the scripture of His day He was pointing to a verbal fulfillment of those scriptures. He saw the scripture that was available to Him as verbally inerrant. He is our example. How dare we understand God's Word in any other way?

To understand the Bible as the literal Word of God gives us the ground by which we can understand it with the full assurance that we have grasped God's purposes, teachings and thoughts. Recognizing the relationship between Covenants and Dispensations within the biblical context is the only means whereby we find no contradictions. It effectively shuts the door to opinions. Is it no wonder that Peter wrote: *"Knowing this first, that no prophecy of the scripture is of any private interpretation."* (II Peter 1:20)?

To this point in our study, one covenant has paralleled with one dispensation. As we now move forward we will see that three covenants are embodied in the next dispensation. The primary covenant is the Mosaic Covenant which gives us the dispensational test. There is, however, an important relationship between the Palestinian and Davidic Covenants and this dispensation as we shall see (cf. chart #3).

THE PALESTINIAN AND DAVIDIC COVENANTS

The Palestinian and Davidic Covenants are specifically related to the Jewish people and the nation of Israel. These two covenants more fully explain the first two divine promises found in the Abrahamic Covenant (cf. Chart #3). These provide further details of the first two unconditional promises made by God to Abram and through Abram, to the Jewish people.

Since the Abrahamic Covenant is unconditional, so must the Palestinian and Davidic Covenants be unconditional. Again, as we consider the covenantal formula, we find that there are no conditions related to the expanded provisions given us in these two covenants. Let us examine these covenants more fully.

THE PALESTINIAN COVENANT

The Palestinian Covenant is recorded in Deuteronomy 30:1-10. It amplifies the land features of the Abrahamic Covenant re-affirming to Israel their title deed to the land promised to Abram and his seed forever. There is an interesting point to make here. As one reads the Palestinian Covenant in Deuteronomy it is clear that the land grant given by God to Israel through Abraham, Isaac and Jacob was in perpetuity. However, blessings were promised only as they dwelt in the land. God's gracious returning of Abram's seed to the land is to bring about the ultimate fulfillment of His unconditional promises (blessings).

We note that Israel was removed from the land because of their unfaithfulness (cf. Deuteronomy 28:63-68; 30:1-3). Their return to the land by divine decree will be followed by a yet future repentance of Israel. This will be in relationship to the return of the Messiah to establish His millennial reign. Thus, Israel will be fully restored to the land (Deuteronomy 30:5) at the conclusion of the Great Tribulation. Israel will be converted as a nation (Deuteronomy 30:6; Isaiah 66:7-9). Israel's enemies will be judged (Deuteronomy 30:7). Then will Israel receive her full blessing promised by the Abrahamic Covenant (Deuteronomy 30:9) in the millennial kingdom.

This covenant begins in the dispensation of the Law and continues into eternity. This covenant is the theme of Ezekiel 16. Note especially verses 60-62: *"Nevertheless, I will remember my covenant with thee in the days of thy youth, and I will establish unto thee an everlasting covenant. Then thou shalt remember thy ways, and be ashamed, when thou shalt receive thy sisters, thine elder and thy younger: and I will give them unto thee for daughters, but not by thy covenant. And I will establish my covenant with thee; and thou shalt know that I am the LORD."*

THE DAVIDIC COVENANT

The Davidic Covenant is found in II Samuel 7:12-16. Six times the phrase "I Will" is used by God with not a single conditional "if". This covenant, without question, is unconditional. In this covenant God is enlarging the "seed" promises of the Abrahamic Covenant.

There are four provisions in the Davidic Covenant. David will have a child who will succeed him and establish the promised kingdom (II Samuel 7:12). This son (Solomon) will build the temple that David was not allowed to build (II Samuel 7:13). The throne will not be taken from Solomon though he deserves it (II Samuel 7:14-15). In the final promise God states that the throne of David's kingdom will be established forever (II Samuel 7:16). This promise will be fulfilled when Messiah (the seed of David) returns and establishes the Millennial Kingdom.

This covenant was established with Israel during the dispensation of the law and extends into eternity because it is unconditional.

THE MOSAIC COVENANT

The Mosaic Covenant is found in Exodus 19:5 to Deuteronomy 28:65. The covenant itself extends from Moses to Calvary; from Exodus 19:5 to John 21:25. Much error in biblical teaching would disappear if those seeking to teach God's word only understood that Jesus lived under the Mosaic Law and the dispensation of the Law.

This covenant established a peculiar relationship between God and Israel (the Jewish people). Under this covenant Israel became a uniquely chosen people and nation (Deuteronomy

4:32-40; 7:6-8; 10:14-15; Isaiah 49:15-16). Because of this new relationship Israel became the special receiver of Divine revelation and blessing (Deuteronomy 4:35; Psalm 103:7; 147:19-20). Deuteronomy 28 makes clear that this covenant is conditional as Moses lays out a list of blessings for obedience and a long list of curses for disobedience.

The unique characteristic of the Mosaic Covenant is that it limited man to God Himself requiring perfect (absolute) obedience to all its requirements. It promised blessing to those who kept the whole law and curses to those who did not (cf. Deuteronomy 28).

THE DISPENSATION OF THE LAW

The dispensation of the Law may be called the age of Moses. The period extends from the giving of the law to Moses on Mount Sinai to Christ's death at Calvary. The scripture covered in this dispensation is from Exodus 19:5 to John 19:42. Further helpful information is found in Exodus 34:10-32 which gives us the actual record of the Decalogue being presented to Israel. Please take the time to read this extended passage.

The characteristic of the law was to establish a unique relationship between Israel and God requiring man to perfectly fulfill the law. The value of the law was to teach Israel her helplessness because of sin to bring her to faith in her promised Messiah/Redeemer. Paul made this clear in his letter to the Galatian Church. *"But the scripture hath concluded all under sin that the promise by faith of Jesus Christ might be given to them that believe. But before faith came, we were kept under the law; shut up unto the faith which should afterwards be revealed. Wherefore the law was our schoolmaster to bring us unto Christ, that we might be justified by faith. But after that faith is come, we are no longer under a schoolmaster.* (Galatians 3:22-25). It was never God's intent for the Law to be the means of salvation.

It is helpful to understand what the word "schoolmaster" meant in Paul's day. "A schoolmaster (Gr. paidagogos) is really

43

the trusted boy-leader or child escort employed to attend a boy from six to sixteen to watch over his morals and manners. He was not the teacher and he had no authority to punish. His business was to see that the child went to the right places and did the right things. Such was the purpose of the law, to prescribe right conduct and impose certain checks. The law convicts of sin, restrains from sin, and condemns for sin; but the law cannot save from sin."iv

During the fourteen centuries of the law some believed, not in the ritual of the law, but in the promise of a Saviour. This is clearly the message and testimony of the Old Testament prophets. It was never God's intent for the law to save. His plan of redemption has always been by faith in the shed blood of His Lamb offered up at Calvary. Salvation by Grace through faith, as we have already seen in this study, was God's plan from the beginning.

The reward held out was clear and definite. *"Hear therefore, O Israel, and observe to do it; that it may be well with thee, and that ye may increase mightily, as the LORD God of thy fathers hath promised thee, in the land that floweth with milk and honey."* *(Deuteronomy 6:3)*. The curse threatened was no less specific. *"Cursed be he that confirmeth not all the words of this law to do them.(Deuteronomy 27:26)*. See also Deuteronomy 28:19-20 and Galatians 3:10.

It was man's responsibility to do all of the law (cf. Deuteronomy 5:29-33; Romans 10:5; James 2:10). The test was whether man, limited to his own efforts with detailed regulations governing his conduct in relation to God and his fellow man covering his moral, social and religious activities, is able to lead a holy (sinless) life. Man could not. He was a complete failure under this test. He sinned in every way. *"Understand therefore, that the LORD thy God giveth thee not this good land to possess it for thy righteousness; for thou art a stiffnecked people."* *(Deuteronomy 9:6)*. He goes on to describe the many reasons He described them as stiffnecked as you read on in Deuteronomy 9:7-22.

You may also want to read II Kings 17:7-17. The prophets are full of illustrations of Israel's failures. But the greatest was the crucifixion of their Messiah/Redeemer. *"Ye men of Israel, hear these words; Jesus of Nazareth, a man approved of God among you by miracles and wonders and signs, which God did by him in the midst of you, as ye yourselves also know; Him, being delivered by the determinate counsel and foreknowledge of God, ye have taken, and by wicked hands have crucified and slain." (Acts 2:22-23).* They consistently broke the commandments, disregarded the judgments, and despised the ordinances (example- Exodus 32:1-6). They consistently refused to admit their inability to do that which was right thus refusing God's continuous offer of redemption through faith in the sacrifice that He promised them.

Israel's sins resulted in God's judgment as He sent them into captivity, first the ten tribes into Assyria (II Kings 17:1-8), and later the other two tribes into Babylon (II Kings 25:1-11). Later, a remnant returned to the land under Ezra and Nehemiah. But, when the Messiah came to them, they took responsibility for His death (Matthew 27:25). Therefore they were again cast aside into a worldwide dispersion after the destruction of the Temple and the holy city of Jerusalem.

GOD'S GRACIOUS INTERVENTION

God graciously intervened all through Israel's history during this Age to pardon their rebellions and to withhold the just punishment they deserved. The sacrifices often saved them (cf. Judges 2:1-5; I Chronicles 21:26-27). On several occasions the prayers of Moses availed for them (cf. Exodus 32:1-14). Joshua's pleadings on their behalf were heard (cf. Joshua 7:6 ff). God sent judges to deliver them (cf. Judges 2:16). Their Kings were often helped by God both in battles and in government (cf. I Samuel 30:7-10; II Samuel 5:17-19). They were admonished by the prophets. Protection was divinely given them in Babylon. Even God's protection is still given them to preserve them (example: the holocaust) to this day. Even a future restoration and a final blessing in the Millennium is promised them through the Palestinian and Davidic Covenants. What a gracious God!

CONCLUSIONS

We are seeing that God's revelation of truth is progressive and that it develops within the framework of covenants and dispensations. What are we learning from all of this about God and world history? We are learning that God is in control; that He is working out His program (plan) for the Ages. We are seeing that God, though He is holy (righteous), is a God of love who deals with His creation in Grace. Are you beginning to see that the Bible, both Old and New Testaments, is one book with just one basic message? It is the book of world history that enables us to understand secular history. Only through a thorough study of God's Word, recognizing the importance of dispensations and covenants, will we develop a divine world view giving us the ability to understand God's program for the Ages. Only then will we understand what God is doing right now.

CHAPTER 8

THE NEW COVENANT AND THE DISPENSATION OF GRACE

We have now seen that all biblical truth generates from three foundational truths found in the first three chapters of Genesis, the book of the beginnings. We have learned that biblical truth is developed progressively through the channel of the biblical covenants and dispensations. When properly seen through this channel, there are no contradictions. All truth fits together as one clear message. The only way one can be sure that he has understood God's truth on any specific subject is when the understanding we have of a particular scripture or scriptural subject is found to be in harmony with all other related scriptures. No one doctrine stands alone. Every true biblical doctrine must be seen in relationship with every other doctrine. If, at any point as we study a particular doctrine, there appears to be a contradiction with any other doctrine, we can be assured that we do not have God's mind on the matter.

When we understand that biblical truth flows through the channel of the covenants and dispensations, we are enabled to see even the small issues in the light of the total picture thus understanding God's mind on any matter. Whether we are teaching, preaching, or just reading for our own understanding and growth, we are admonished to be empowered by the Holy Spirit so that what we share goes forth in the power and authority of "thus saith the Lord." This takes a solid understanding of God's program for the ages. The further progression of that program is found in the New Covenant and its relationship to the Dispensation of Grace.

In relation to the previous dispensation and related covenants we noted that once again man failed the test but that God graciously intervened. The Mosaic Covenant was conditional.

Yet God showed Grace for hundreds of years before He finally brought this test to an end by graciously sending the promised Messiah as the ultimate sacrifice ending the necessity for the Mosaic Covenant. As we turn now to a study of the New Covenant and the related Dispensation of Grace, we shall see that the Abrahamic covenant will ultimately and finally be fulfilled (Note Chart #3).

THE NEW COVENANT

The New Covenant encompasses the final two dispensations (see chart #3). There are many scriptures that deal with this covenant. However, it is clearly laid out in Jeremiah 31:31-34. As you read this passage, take special notice that six times God states: "I will." As there is no use of the phrase "If you", it is clear that this covenant is unconditional. The fulfillment of this covenant is dependent upon God keeping His promises, not upon man doing anything.

THE COVENANT FEATURES

There are eight specific features in this covenant. God said: *"I will put my law in their inward parts, and write it in their hearts* (Jeremiah 31:33b). God states His purpose for this in Ezekiel 11:19-20 where He states: *That they may walk in my statutes, and keep mine ordinances, and do them."* He promises to give them a new heart that will transform them. This speaks both of individual and national regeneration (cf. Ezekiel 36:24-32).

God promises that they will be restored to favor and blessing. He states: *"And I will be their God, and they shall be my people"* (Jeremiah 31:33c) (cf. Isaiah 66:7-9). It is an interesting fact that Moses spoke of this very time when he said: *"And the LORD thy God will circumcise thine heart, and the heart of thy seed, to love the LORD thy God with all thine heart, and with all thy soul, that thou mayest live"* (Deuteronomy 30:6).

This covenant promises regeneration, restoration and forgiveness of sins. God said: *"For I will forgive their iniquity, and*

I will remember their sins no more" (Jeremiah 31:34c). Further He promises them that He will give them His Spirit (Holy Spirit) to indwell and teach (cf. Ezekiel 36:27; Jeremiah 31:33a).

Material blessings are promised (cf. Ezekiel 39:26-29). The Temple will be rebuilt (cf. Ezekiel 37:25-28; Chapters 40-44). When all of this shall come to pass Universal peace will be established (cf. Isaiah 11;6-9).

There is one further promise that is inherent here. That is the promise of the shedding of Messiah's blood to make all of this possible. Dwight Pentecost stated: "This covenant is based on blood. The New Covenant guarantees Israel a converted heart as the foundation of all her blessings. According to the Old Testament principle, this type of conversion cannot be permanently affected without the shedding of blood. This covenant makes necessary as its foundation a sacrifice acceptable to God."[v] Leviticus 17:11 requires it: *"For the life of the flesh is in the blood: and I have given it to you upon the altar to make an atonement for your souls: for it is the blood that maketh an atonement for the soul."* This again demonstrates that the heart of God's program for the ages is the "exchange of life" principle established with Adam after he had sinned. The basis of the nation's redemption and all other blessings is clearly stated in Zechariah 12:10 where God stated: *"And I will pour upon the House of David, and upon the inhabitants of Jerusalem, the spirit of grace and supplications: and they shall look upon me whom they have pierced, and they shall mourn for him, as one mourneth for his only son, and shall be in bitterness for his firstborn."* At the conclusion of the outpouring of God's wrath upon this earth in what we know as the Tribulation, the Jews who survive long enough to see Messiah return in glory will repent of their sin and *"they shall call on my name, and I will hear them: I will say, It is my people: they shall say, The LORD is my God"* (Zechariah 13:9c).

But what is His name? Isaiah tells us His name in Isaiah 62:11. *"Behold, the LORD hath proclaimed unto the end of the world, Say ye to the daughter of Zion, Behold, thy salvation cometh; behold, his reward is with him, and his work before him."* Notice that "salvation" here is not a concept. It is a person. The Hebrew word is "Yasha" or "Yesha" and is a root for Yeshua which literally means "Jehovah saves". Years ago I was on a television broadcast in Clearwater, Florida with a Rabbi (his broadcast). We were talking about Jesus when he said to me: "If Jesus is our Messiah, why was He not named in our scriptures?" After I read Isaiah 62:11 to him I asked: "What is the Hebrew word translated salvation?" He immediately replied: "Yeshua". Then I asked him who was the "his, him, his, him" of this verse pointing out that the antecedent to these pronouns could not be a concept but a person. You may want to look at Isaiah 12:2 and Psalm 118:21 as well.

Thus the features of this covenant are: regeneration, restoration, forgiveness, the gift of the indwelling Holy Spirit, material blessings, the Temple rebuilt, universal peace established, all based upon the foundation of the shed blood of the Messiah. This covenant amplifies the third part of the Abrahamic Covenant (cf. Chart #3). When we later consider the final dispensation we will see that it will be the final time block completing God's Program for the Ages.

THE DISPENSATION OF GRACE

Any study of the New Covenant will show that the fulfillment of this covenant historically falls into two time periods. From the standpoint of time, the Dispensation of Grace covers the first period of the New Covenant. It is important to note that the Age of Grace and the Church Age are not interchangeable terms. The Church Age is included in the Dispensation of Grace. The Church Age begins at Pentecost when the Church was empowered giving it life and concludes with the Rapture when it is caught away. The Age of Grace, in general, is that of the Lord Jesus Christ. The period extends from Christ's resurrection to the beginning of His millennial reign. It covers the major portion of the New Testament. Within the biblical account, the

Age of Grace begins with the resurrection accounts and covers everything to Revelation 20:21.

The state of man during this period is that he is constituted a helpless sinner. This is set forth in scripture embodying three aspects. First, we are told that sin is imputed to man through Adam's sin. *"Wherefore, as by one man sin entered into the world, and death by sin; and so death passed upon all men, for that all have sinned."* (Romans 5:12). The word "impute" means to ascribe or attribute to. When Adam sinned, in him all mankind sinned. The proof of this premise is seen in that as the wages of sin is death (Genesis 2:17), and that death now reigns over all men, as all men in Adam are sinners.

Sin is not only imputed to man because of Adam, but, because of Adam's sin, his fallen nature is transmitted to all men. As we have already seen, when Adam sinned, he died immediately in terms of his relationship with his Creator. This is spiritual death. But he also began to die physically. His physical death is recorded in Genesis 5:5. *"And all the days that Adam lived were nine hundred and thirty years: and he died."* In Genesis 5:3 we are told that Adam *"begat a son in his own likeness, after his image."* Paul confirms that in Adam's seed the fallen (Adamic) nature is passed on (cf. Ephesians 2:3). Jesus clearly stated this in His statement to Nicodemus. *"Verily, verily, I say unto thee, except a man be born of water and of the Spirit, he cannot enter into the kingdom of God."* (John 3:5). Because we are born in Adam's image (water), to be alive to God, we must further be born of the Spirit (redemption). Thus, sin is not only imputed to us, it is also transmitted to us (cf. Romans 7:17-23; I Corinthians 15:21-22). It is also true that man's estate is that of being constituted under sin by divine decree (Romans 3:1-12). So we are sinners because it is imputed and transmitted and divinely decreed.

In this dispensation, man's clearly defined responsibility is to recognize himself as a lost sinner and "to believe on the Lord Jesus Christ" as the only hope of redemption (Acts 16:3-31; Acts 4:12). Man is thereby tested as to whether he will accept the gift of: righteousness (Romans 5:15-18; I Corinthians 1:30), life (Romans 6:23), and the Holy Spirit (Acts 2:38-39) and thus become a member of Christ's body.

Second, as a believer, he is tested as to whether he will cooperate with God in the evangelization of the world, not for the gain or loss of his salvation, but for the gain or loss of rewards (Luke 24:47-48; Acts 1:8; I Corinthians 4:8-15). James tells us that works are an indicator of the reality of our relationship with God established through Christ. It was Jesus who said: *"He that hath my commandments, and keepeth them, he it is that loveth me"* (John 14:21).

Man is without excuse, as God gives all the empowerment needed. Man has a conscience to help him discern between right and wrong; the restraint of the Holy Spirit; human government; unconditional promises; His grace; and the indwelling of His Holy Spirit (Acts 1:8). Does it work? No! Why not? Though a saved man has everything needed to overcome the drawing of his sinful nature he, still at times, chooses sin.

Man has been a miserable failure on both counts. Two thirds of the world's population does not even know His Name. After more than one hundred-fifty years of the modern missionary movement, today, there are more heathen than when the movement began. Consider the apostasy of the professing church even in its early days (cf. Luke 17:26-30; 18:8; II Timothy 3:1-5).

Third, as a judgment, the superficially religious unconverted church members and the Christ-rejecting world at the end of this age will be brought into great tribulation (II Thessalonians 2:1-12; Revelation chapters 4 through 19). This also includes the judgments of Revelation 19:17-21. But, again God will graciously intervene on behalf of His own (the church, Christ's Bride) taking them to Himself, enabling them to escape any portion of the Tribulation (I Thessalonians 4:13-18). This is the intervention of grace for this dispensation.

Why is it impossible for God to allow the church to go through any portion of the Tribulation? The Tribulation is the outpouring of God's wrath upon the unbelieving world. He has promised that those who are His will not experience His wrath (Romans 5:9; I Thessalonians 1:10; 5:9; Revelation 3:10). God's grace is also seen in the fact that the human race will not be totally blotted out (cf. Matthew 24:22). It is further seen by the multitude who will be saved out of the Tribulation (cf. Revelation chapter 7). (For a more complete study of this subject see the author's book entitled "The Blessed Hope".)

CONCLUSIONS

The Dispensation of Grace covers the first period of the implementation of the New Covenant, a time when the church, the called-out body of believers in Jesus the Messiah, is the prominent institution. There are seven clear references to the New Covenant in relation to the church: Matthew 26:28; Mark 14:24; Luke 22:20; I Corinthians 11:25; II Corinthians 3:6; Hebrews 8:8; 9:15. There are three other references where the relationship is implied: Romans 11:27; Hebrews 8:10-13; 12:24.

All of the major biblical covenants are instituted with a blood sacrifice. Jesus so stated as it is recorded in Matthew 26:28. The author of Hebrews stated it several times. Consider Hebrews 8:7-13. Speaking of Jesus he wrote: *"For this cause he is the mediator of the New Testament* (covenant), *that by means of death, for the redemption of the transgressions that were under the first testament, they which are called might receive the promise of eternal inheritance"* (Hebrews 9:15). He further stated: *"And to Jesus the mediator of the new covenant, and to the blood of sprinkling, that speaketh better things than that of Abel"* (Hebrews 12:24). Again, speaking of Jesus, he wrote: *"Then said he, Lo, I come to do thy will, O God. He taketh away the first, that he may establish the second. By the which will we are sanctified through the offering of the body of Jesus Christ once for all"* (Hebrews 10:9-10). We see not only the connection between the Age of Grace and the New Covenant, but note that the New Covenant is instituted by the sacrifice of Jesus, God's Son, at Calvary. Thus, before the final act of God's revelation, He brings His plan full circle to where He began with just one, Adam, through whom He included all, and went back to one, Abram, through whom He also has included all through just one man, Jesus, the second Adam!

Before we close this chapter, we must deal with one question often asked: "What of the tribulation saints? Are they a part of the church? The answer is that they are not any more than the Old Testament saints were a part of the church. The true church (true believers) is caught out before the Tribulation begins. After Revelation Chapter three the church is not mentioned again except in heaven until they come back with Christ at His second coming.

Our theme has been progressive revelation. It is interesting to note, as we have in this chapter, that with each new dispensation, the resources of the previous dispensations are still available to us along with at least one new resource to enable us to be what God intended from the beginning for us to be. This emphasizes the importance of understanding the flow of God's revelation of His plan for the ages. For, how can we understand His present dealings with man, if we have not come to understand how we got to where we now are?

CHAPTER 9

THE NEW COVENANT AND THE DISPENSATION OF THE MILLENIUM

It is important for us to understand that the New Covenant embraces both the Dispensation of Grace and the Dispensation of the Millennium. In the previous chapter we noted that the Dispensation of Grace covers the first part of the New Covenant. In this chapter we will deal with the relationship between the New Covenant and the Dispensation of the Millennium.

We have noted that, in the Dispensation of Grace, God is dealing with all mankind in three areas: regeneration, forgiveness of sins, and the gift of the indwelling Holy Spirit to both teach and empower the believer to be what God has intended us to be. This work is accomplished by God through the gift of His Son, Israel's Messiah, whose blood was shed as the full and complete payment for sin. In this dispensation the test for all people, Jewish or Gentile, is whether they will recognize themselves as lost sinners and accept God's payment made on their behalf for their sin.

We further noted that it was Messiah's (Jesus') sacrifice of Himself that instituted the New Covenant. This is a truth that has been totally missed by Judaism and even by many Christians who do not understand that God's redemptive plan for all mankind was provided by God through the Jewish people (the seed of Abraham).

Now, as we conclude this study of God's Plan for the Ages, we must consider the personal millennial reign of Israel's Messiah in righteousness which leads to the final establishment of the new heaven and the new earth. We shall see that the millennial kingdom concludes with eternity.

55

THE DISPENSATION OF THE MILLENNIUM

The Dispensation of the Millennium includes part of the day of the Lord (I Thessalonians chapter 5). In his study of this chapter Dr. Walvoord, as does Dr. Dwight Pentecost, defines the Day of The Lord as beginning with the Rapture and "includes all the end-time as well as the thousand year reign of Christ itself."vi The Millennium extends from the beginning of the reign of Israel's Messiah/King to the end of the millennium which will conclude with the Great White Throne judgment. It is called a millennium because it is prophesied to last one thousand years (Revelation 20:1-10). The passages describing this dispensation are scattered throughout both the Old and New Testaments but conclude in Revelation 20:1-15.

The characteristic of this age will be righteousness enforced by the personal reign of Christ, Who will rule with a rod of iron (cf. Revelation 2:27; 12:5; 19:15). As one studies the Messianic prophesies from the Old Testament, there is only one person in history who fulfills all of the prophesies related to the first coming of the Messiah. He would come as a suffering servant, suffer and die as the divine payment for the sins of all mankind (cf. Isaiah 53). Jesus is the only one who claimed to be the Messiah who meets all the qualifications. You will find a more complete study of this truth in chapter 17 of J. Dwight Pentecost's book entitled *Thy Kingdom Come.*

The Gospel of Matthew presents Jesus as Israel's Messiah/King. Jesus offered Israel the Kingdom, but they rejected the offer and crucified Him. In Revelation 19:15 it is Jesus who returns to claim His kingdom, establishing it and ruling with a firm hand. Micah 4:7, Zephaniah 3:15 and Zechariah 14:9, among other scriptures, show that the Messiah/King is the Lord Himself. That is the very message with which John begins his Gospel: *"In the beginning was the word, and the word was with God, and the word was God. The same was in the beginning with God. All things were made by him; and without him was not anything made that was made....And the word was made flesh and dwelt among us (and we beheld his glory, the glory as of the only begotten of the Father,) full of grace and truth"* (John 1:1 -3, 14). This is the very message of the prophets stated over and over again (cf. Daniel 9:25-27, etc.). This one who comes to be "King of Kings and Lord of Lords" is none other than Jesus, the God/Man, the last Adam (I Corinthians 15:45-50).

The special test to which man will be subject is: Will man live righteously when Satan is bound and Christ and His redeemed ones are personally present and reigning in righteousness on the earth? The Sermon on the Mount and other similar passages set forth the method of conduct and responsibility (cf. Matthew chapters 5-7). Disobedience will be visited with prompt and exact judgment.

During His ministry, Jesus proclaimed the Gospel of the Kingdom (Matthew 4:23). Again and again He proclaimed that the Kingdom was coming. It was necessary that the Kingdom promised be offered to Israel, the seed of Abraham through Isaac and Jacob (cf. Chart #3-features). The Kingdom message was exclusively for Israel, for the Jew. In their acceptance of the Kingdom offer, they would be accepting the King and the redemption He would bring through His sacrifice according to the promises made by God in the covenants previously established with Israel. Had Israel received the Kingdom when it was offered there would have been no need for the Church Age. With the coming of the Church Age, the message changed, because now the target group was the whole world. The message to the world remains the same as it has always been since Adam fell. Salvation is through faith in the shed blood of God's lamb, Israel's Messiah. So today, in the Church Age, we proclaim the death, burial and resurrection of Jesus, God's Lamb.

Man's failure is prophesied in that after the one thousand year reign , Satan, having been loosed, will be able to gather a multitude to join him in his attack upon the camp of the saints (Revelation 20:7-9). It thus appears that, even though conditions are almost as paradise, many simply conform, not out of a heart of love for the Messiah/King, but of the fear of immediate judgment for any act of rebellion. This is the final proof that redemption is not gained by conformity to the law, but by a changed heart brought about when man recognizes that he is lost without hope and accepts God's offer of grace through faith in Jesus Christ. The resultant judgment of the incorrigible wicked will be their destruction by fire from heaven. *"And they went up on the breadth of the earth, and compassed the camp of the saints about, and the beloved city; and fire came down from God out of heaven, and devoured them. And the devil that had deceived them was cast into the lake of fire and brimstone; where the beast and the false prophet are, and shall be tormented day and night forever and ever"* (Revelation 20:9-10).

Grace will have provided, by means of the dispensational dealings of God with man, every conceivable test to show man completely that he is lost and how absolutely without hope he is apart from God's Grace. Thus there is no gracious intervention recorded for the conclusion of this final dispensation, unless the eternal separation of the incorrigible wicked from Himself be so considered (cf. Revelation 20:11-15).

CONCLUSIONS

The incorrigible wicked of all ages are finally judged for all eternity. God creates a new heaven and a new earth. All tears at this point are wiped away (Revelation 21:4). Revelation 21:9-22:7 describes for us the New Jerusalem that begins for the saints during the Millennial Kingdom and continues into eternity. During the Millennial Kingdom the saints have access to the earth, as those who have met the conditions will assist Christ in His millennial rule (cf. Revelation 2:26-27).

LIFE IN THE ETERNAL CITY

Life in the eternal city will be characterized by eight qualities of life. The saints will have perfect fellowship with the Triune God. John stated the promise this way: *"Beloved, now are we the sons of God, and it doth not yet appear what we shall be: but we know that, when he shall appear, we shall be like him, for we shall see him as he is"* (I John 3:2). As all sin shall have been removed, our fellowship with our Lord will be unhindered for all eternity.

According to Revelation 14:13, we shall have a perfect rest.. *"And I heard a voice out of heaven saying unto me, write, blessed are the dead which die in the Lord from henceforth: Yea, saith the Spirit, that they may rest from their labours; and their works do follow them."* The word "henceforth" refers to a coming day. The promise is that a day is coming when we as His children will be forever set free from the trials and tribulations of this earthly life (the labours). Our activities in the New Jerusalem and eternity will be joyful and a blessing. Ours will be a perfect rest.

Third, we will have perfect knowledge. Paul said: *"For now we see through a glass darkly; but then face to face: Now I know in part; but then shall I know even as I am known"* (I Corinthians 13:12). This takes us all the way back to Genesis three and the serpent's big lie as he told Eve that God was holding out on her. God's intention, from the very beginning, was to reveal all truth to man. But man had to be prepared for each new revelation. God's plan for the ages prepared man for that ultimate revelation. Can it be any wonder that we will be grateful that we have an eternity to be grateful?

In the New Jerusalem we will know perfect joy. *"And I heard a great voice out of heaven saying, behold, the tabernacle of God is with men, and he will dwell with them, and they shall be his people, and God himself shall be with them, and be their God"* (Revelation 21:3). From the very beginning it was God's intention to fellowship with man. For that purpose did He create us. David wrote: *"In thy presence is fullness of joy"* (Psalm 16:11). Notice that "fullness of Joy" is determined by our relationship with God, our Creator, the new birth. Happiness is determined by outward circumstances, but joy is determined by a right relationship with our Creator/God. In eternity that relationship will be perfect. Thus our joy will be consistently full for all eternity.

59

We also will enjoy perfect service. John wrote: *"And there shall be no more curse; but the throne of God and of the Lamb shall be in it; and his servants shall serve him"* (Revelation 22:3). What a joy it will be to serve Him who gave His all for us that we might have eternal life.

There will be perfect abundance. Revelation 21:6 promises us that the water of life shall be freely given. Revelation 22:2 promises not only what we need to eat, but the leaves will be for the "healing of the nations". Every need will be provided. We will enjoy perfect abundance.

We shall know perfect glory. *"For our light affliction, which is but for a moment, worketh for us a far more exceeding and eternal weight of glory, while we look not at the things which are seen, but at the things which are not seen; for the things which are seen are temporal; but the things which are not seen are eternal"* (II Corinthians 4:17-18). We will dwell in the glory of the living and eternal God, our Lord and Saviour. We will know perfect glory.

Finally, we will also experience perfect worship. This is the message of Revelation 19:1-6. Worship is living in His presence, giving Him all the glory and honor due unto His Name. *"And I heard as it were the voice of a great multitude, and as the voices of many waters, and as the voice of mighty thunderings; saying, Alleluia: for the Lord God omnipotent reigneth"* (Revelation 19:6). We will have a perfect relationship with our God and Saviour. Thus we will know and experience perfect worship. We will know perfect fellowship, perfect rest, perfect knowledge, perfect joy, perfect service, perfect abundance, perfect glory, and perfect worship. We shall be fully occupied with the one who loved us; who hath washed us from our sins with His own precious blood, and hath made us kings and priests unto God and His Father (cf. Revelation 1:5-6).

As God's plan for the Ages comes to its conclusion, He has brought man full circle. That which He had intended for Adam in the garden and for all mankind has now become a reality. God has not failed to accomplish His purpose. He is the only one and true God.

CHAPTER 10

GOD'S PROGRAM FOR THE AGES

As we conclude this study, let us consider God's program for the Ages. The driving principle for His program is based on the truth that God created man for fellowship. He created man in His own image so that man would be free to have fellowship with his Creator/God. In order for two people to have true fellowship both must be free to choose to do so. The Bible, then, is the story of God's relationship with His creation, including man. Thus one cannot fully understand history apart from understanding His story. Coming to grasp this truth enables us to have a proper world view. God is in control of all history working out His redemptive program. The basic principle of God's program for the Ages is based upon His desire to have fellowship with man.

In order to accomplish this fellowship God had to establish a circumstance whereby man could exercise freedom to choose. He made man's environment perfect. Man wanted for nothing. Until man rebelled, that fellowship was perfect. The relationship between God and man in the garden was beautiful and perfect. They walked together enjoying one another. But sin brought death; first spiritual death and then physical death. Man's sin created the need for a plan whereby God could redeem man; a plan that would overcome the effects of sin restoring that much desired fellowship.

God immediately provided a plan for man's redemption based upon the "exchange of life" principle. Man was (and continues to be) incapable on his own of recapturing his sinless state. God's righteousness demanded a perfect sacrifice. God knew that "the life of the flesh is in the blood." Thus He knew that He had to provide in His mercy and grace a perfect sacrifice, a sacrifice that He immediately informed man about and symbolized it by providing them a temporary "covering" until the sacrifice would be offered. This plan of redemption was progressively developed through covenants and dispensations making it necessary to understand both dispensations and covenants and their relationship to each other.

The story of the Bible, then, is a story of God's grace in providing that redemption for man. It involves a series of tests, the purpose of which is to demonstrate to man his inability to provide his own redemption, while still holding out the great blessings to man of having fellowship with God. This program involves seven dispensations (time periods) with each embodying a test, the purpose of which is to show man his lost estate and inability to correct it while holding out to man His redemptive plan to them if they would but receive it by faith.

In relation to each dispensation, God established with man eight covenants that span the period of world history. The emphasis of the covenants was the requirements for fellowship with the blessings for obedience always held out. Thus, God's redemptive program flows in a channel between covenants and dispensations for the purpose of bringing man to the place where he will admit that he is totally without hope apart from God's grace offered through the perfect sacrifice of His Lamb (the Lord Jesus) and be moved to reach out in faith to receive that gift of redemption.

Each dispensation builds upon the previous dispensation as do the covenants. First, there was a perfect environment. Man's sin gave him the knowledge of good and evil which instituted within him a conscience to guide him to choose good over evil. Then God established the basis for human government to give further motivation to choose good over evil with the establishment of the death penalty for murder. With the dispensation of promise God again chose one man and his family and promised them great material, social and spiritual blessings if they would choose to do right. Law was instituted to reveal to them their sin and God's judgments upon it. In Grace God offered a transformed heart and the indwelling presence of His Spirit. During the Millennium the Messiah will rule with a rod of iron while Satan is bound in the abyss. His followers on earth will be restrained while peace and justice prevail on earth. In all of these tests, some respond, but most do not. Now, at the conclusion of all of these tests man stands in God's presence without any excuse and God's righteousness is vindicated as He judges those of all ages who were rebellious and evil.

From the moment of man's fall, God established that salvation (redemption) could be received only by faith in the perfect sacrifice that God Himself would provide on man's behalf. History revolves around three men: Adam, Abraham and Jesus, the Christ. In Adam all sinned thus creating a conflict between good and evil. Beginning with Abraham God's plan has essentially revolved around His dealings with Israel and the Jewish people, Abraham's descendents through Isaac and Jacob. Even though God's focus was upon Abraham and His designated seed, the whole world has been affected because Israel was to take the message of redemption to the whole world (cf. the book of Jonah). The unconditional aspects of each covenant became a part of the succeeding covenants. All of this culminates with the conclusion of the Millennial Kingdom with God again establishing an eternal kingdom with those from all ages who have responded to Him in faith.

Covenants and dispensations are not mutually exclusive. They are two compatible parts of the whole program with covenants emphasizing the issues of relationship and dispensations emphasizing the role of time. In the end, we see the Bible as one book, God's love letter to man.

The Bible is God's Word. Jesus understood the scriptures available to Him (the Old Testament) as the verbally inerrant word of God. He took it literally. This study has shown us that this is the only way to make sense of it without any contradictions. Jesus, the Son of God, set for us the pattern.

In this study we have considered the development of God's Plan for the Ages. We have learned that He is in control every step of the way. We have researched and laid out the umbilical cord of His plan, the development of the key truths. We have learned that God's revelation is progressive and flows easily between two concepts: biblical covenants and biblical dispensations between which there is no contradiction. We have noted that five of the covenants are specifically related to Israel. In four of those covenants, there are unconditional promises made only to Israel and the Jewish people making it clear that God, if He is God, is not finished either with the Jew or Israel also making it clear that the Church is not Israel thus making the church of this age responsible for taking to them the Gospel of Salvation. Every biblical doctrine or truth fits within this fundamental program without any contradiction either to the plan or to any other truth. The challenge to the reader now is to read your Bible with this understanding. His truth can be known with all assurance as we fit everything into His fundamental program for the Ages. Let's not worry about being theologians. Let us just be Biblicists! If we will just be Biblicists theology will take care of itself. The Bible is God's infallible word without error or contradiction. Here is God's program for the Ages. It can help you know the truth that will set you free. Lay aside your preconceived ideas. Just accept the clear truth of His Word. And it will all begin to make sense and thus be a blessing to your heart.

There is a world that needs the truth embodied in this sacred book, the Bible. Let us be about the business of understanding and sharing it with a lost and dying world.

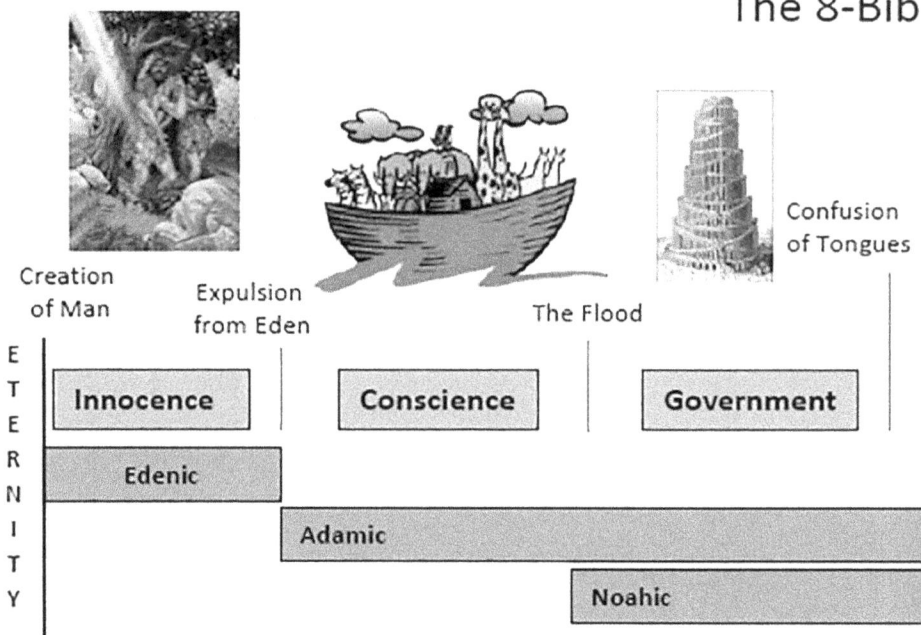

Confusion
of Tongues

Creation
of Man

Expulsion
from Eden

The Flood

E
T
E
R
N
I
T
Y

Innocence	Conscience	Government

| Edenic | | |

| Adamic | | |

| Noahic | |

Dispensation: Period of time God deals with man in a distinct way with respect to man's responsibilities before God.

Covenant: A binding agreement between God and man; some of these are conditional, while others are unconditional.

Innocence	Conscience	Human Government	Call
Mans Creation through Mans fall	Mans fall through flood	After flood through Tower of Babel	
Gen 1:28-3:24	Gen 4:1-8:14	Gen 8:15-11:9	

Edenic	Adamic	Noahic	Abraham
Mans Creation through Mans fall	Mans fall through Earths End	After flood through Earths End	Call of Abral through all et
Gen 2:15-28	Gen 3:14-19	Gen 9:11-16	Gen 12:1-15
Conditional	Unconditional	Unconditional	Unconditio

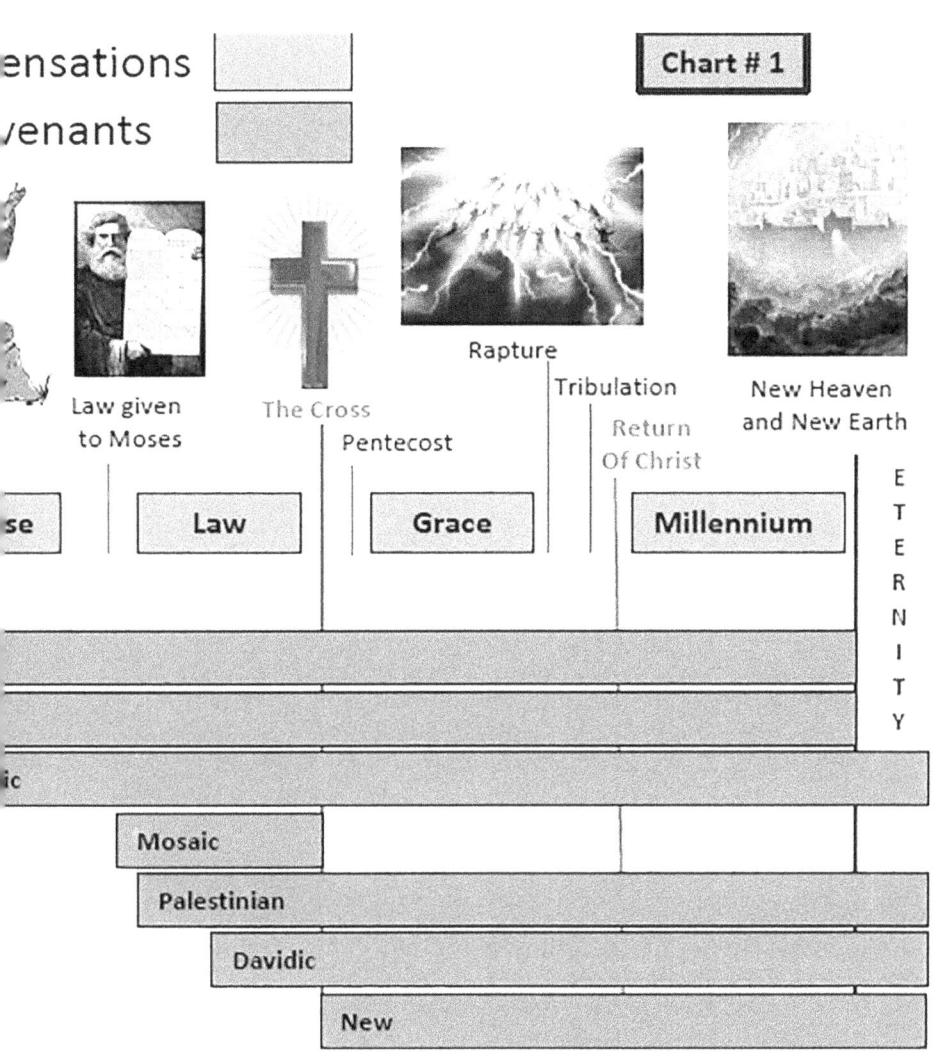

ensations

venants

Chart # 1

Rapture

Tribulation

New Heaven
and New Earth

Law given
to Moses

The Cross

Pentecost

Return
Of Christ

se

Law

Grace

Millennium

E T E R N I T Y

ic

Mosaic

Palestinian

Davidic

New

	Law	Grace of God	Kingdom/Millennium
Mosaic	Mount Sinai though Mount Calvary	Pentecost through return of Christ	Return of Christ through 1000 year Millennium
8:27	Ex 19:1-Jn 19:42	Acts 2:1- Rev 19	Rev 20:1-7

Mosaic	Palestinian	Davidic	New
nt Sinai through the Cross	In Wilderness through all eternity	King David through all eternity	The Cross through all eternity
9:1-Deut 28:65	Deut 29:1-30:9	2 Sam 7:10-16	Jer 31:31-34
Conditional	Unconditional	Unconditional	Unconditional

Chart # 2

FULL UND

G

PROG

REV

IS

28

DESPENSATIONS

FOUNDATIO

STANDING

'S

SSIVE

TION

H

10

COVENANTS

_ PRECEPTS

BASIC COVENANT WITH ABRAHAM STATED		EXPLAINED	FEATURES
The Promise of a National Land Gen 12:1 Gen 13:14,15,17	L A N D	Palestinian Covenant Deut 30:1-5 Ezek 20:33-37 Ezek 20:42-44	1. Israel dispersed (unfaithful) 2. Future repentance 3. Messiah to return 4. Restored to the land 5. Converted 6. Enemies judged 7. Israel fully blessed
The Promise of Numerous Descendants Gen 12:2 Gen 13:16 Gen 17:2-6	S E E D	Davidic Covenant II Sam 7:11,13,16 Jer 33:20,21 Jer 31:35-37	1. A child to establish His kingdom 2. A temple built for the worship of God 3. Throne of His kingdom established forever 4. David's house, throne, kingdom established forever
The Promise of redemption National and Universal Gen 12:3 Gen 22:18 Gal 3:16	B L E S S I N G	New Covenant Jer 31:31-40 Heb 8:6-13	1. Regeneration 2. Restoration to favor and blessing 3. Forgiveness of sins 4. Holy Spirit given to indwell and teach 5. Material blessing 6. Temple rebuilt 7. Universal peace established 8. Blood of Messiah shed
GOD'S UNCONDITIONAL COVENANTS WITH ISRAEL			19 =

	BEING FULFILLED		TO BE FULFILLED		Chart # 3
d	Israel Preserved As A Nation	Israel witnesses the judgment of her enemies		1. Regathered 2. Installed in land 3. Repentant	
				4. Converted as a nation 5. Material blessings given	
f		1. Israel forgiven and given a new heart 2. Temple rebuilt 3. Indwelling, teaching Holy Spirit 4. Universal peace established		Return of Messiah to effect salvation, restoration and blessing of national Israel **The Millennial Kingdom**	
+	4 +	5	+	5 +	1

End Note References

i   Charles C. Ryrie, *Dispensations* (Moody Press, Chicago, 1995) p.33

ii   Arthur W. Pink, Gleanings in Genesis (moody Press, Chicago, 1922) vol. 1, pg 136

iii   ibid

iv   Jerry Falwell, Liberty Bible Commentary (The Old Time Gospel Hour 1982) Vol II, pg 522

v   J. Dwight Pentecost, *Thy Kingdom Come* (Kregel Publications, Grand Rapids, MI, 1995) p. 169

vi   John F. Walvoord, *Major Bible Prophecies* (Zondervan Publishing House, Grand Rapids, MI, 1991) P. 271

BIBLIOGRAPHY

Chafer, Lewis S., *Major Bible Themes*. Grand Rapids: Dunham Publishing Co. 1953

Diprose, Ronald E., *Israel And The Church*. Waynesboro: Authentic Media, 2004

Fruchtenbaum. Arnold G., *The footsteps of the Messiah*. San Antonio: Ariel Ministries, 1982

Hartill, J. Edwin, *Principles of Biblical Hermeneutics*. Grand Rapids: Zondervan Publishing House 1947

Pentecost, J, Dwight, *Thy Kingdom Come*. Grand Rapids: Kregel Publications 1995

Pentecost, J. Dwight, *Things To Come*. Grand Rapids: Dunham Publishing Co. 1958

Pink, Arthur W., *Gleanings in Genesis,* Vol. 1. Chicago: Moody Press 1922

Showers, Renald E., *There Really Is A Difference*. Bellmawr: Friends Of Israel 1990

Walvoord, John F., *Major Bible Prophecies*. Grand Rapids: Zondervan Publishing House 1991

Wurz, Ervin W., *The Life of Abraham*. Taylorsville: Bible Truth Publishing Co. 1973